Branding for Nonprofits:

Developing Identity with Integrity

DK Holland

ALLWORTH PRESS
NEW YORK

D M I

DESIGN MANAGEMENT INSTITUTE

© 2006 DK Holland

10 09 08 07 06   5 4 3 2 1

Published by Allworth Press
An imprint of Allworth Communications, Inc.
10 East 23rd Street, New York, NY 10010

Cover and interior design by Whitehouse & Company, New York
Typography by SR Desktop Services, Ridge, NY

ISBN: 1-58115-434-8

Library of Congress Cataloging-in-Publication Data
Holland, DK.
    Branding for nonprofits : developing identity with integrity /
DK Holland.
        p.   cm.
    Includes index.
        1. Brand name products.   2. Nonprofit organizations—
Marketing.   I. Title.

HD69.B7H645   2006
658.8'27—dc22
                                                    2005026430

Printed in Canada

Dedication

In 1831, while the young Alexis de Tocqueville traveled the rough terrain of our fledgling United States, he witnessed the remarkable optimism, energy, and faith of the people he met along the way. The notion that change was possible against the odds was palpable. Later, in *Democracy in America*, he told the world about this phenomenon—this uniquely American can-do attitude, an attitude that would soon become part of the brand of the United States of America.

The nonprofit and branding systems are also, not coincidentally, unique to the United States. And this book is dedicated to those Americans of the twenty-first century who are the future of nonprofits: those generous, creative, savvy Americans who will use the force of optimism—and their branding skills—to push the world forward.

Contents

Acknowledgments

A phone call in the winter of 2003 led me to Mitch Nauffts, editor of *Philanthropy News Digest* (PND), the online publication of The Foundation Center. I had conducted two seminars there on branding for nonprofits that had been very well received and suggested to him that I follow up by writing an article, and he said, to my delight, "How about an ongoing column?"

My first thought was that it would be best to present the process of branding chronologically and explore a phase in each column so that the reader would better grasp the importance of sequencing in the stages of development. "It would make a good book," I said. Having produced over a dozen books on design, I had no problem imagining it. So thanks to Mitch for his support as "Nonprofits by Design" rolled out online over the course of two years. His skeptical mind and keen editing skills made a big difference to this book.

Thanks to Judie Gilmore for her help and endless enthusiasm for this project. Her insatiable curiosity and commitment to social change gives me hope for the future.

Thanks to Ed Pusz, design director at the Museum of Modern Art, for providing the foreword for this book. MoMA was the first nonprofit brand I chose to interview for my online column and it remains the pinnacle of nonprofit branding, as far as I'm concerned.

Thanks to my sisters, Jennifer and Cecelia Holland, for their help in chapter 12, "On the Evolution of Branding" (the only chapter in the book that did not appear in PND).

When most of the columns were online, I contacted Tad Crawford, president of Allworth Press, publisher of virtually all the books I have ever published and a longtime good friend and ally. I thank Tad for once again having the confidence to see this book through to the marketplace.

Thanks for my longtime colleagues and dear friends, graphic designers Roger Whitehouse, Ben Whitehouse, and Saki Tanaka, for the inspired design of the cover and interior of this book.

Finally, thanks to all the readers of PND's "Nonprofits by Design"—especially those who contacted me to say that the column was providing them with important resources and support. It is for them that I created this book.

DK Holland

New York, N.Y.

Foreword

In one of my earliest meetings with Terence Riley, chief curator of the architecture and design department, he interrupted a presentation to inform me, "Here at the Museum of Modern Art, we don't use the word 'brand.' We prefer the term 'spirit.'" At first I found his statement a semantic matter that comes along with understanding your client's language. Through many years of archival research and countless hours of listening to the oral history of the Museum, I've come to see the wisdom of his words.

What can be found at the heart of all successful nonprofits, regardless of size, is the motivational force of intention. Shared intention, otherwise know as "the mission," binds together dedicated individuals with a common desire to effect positive change on the world around us. This spirit of intention is the mark of a great company— nonprofit or otherwise—and it invigorates the entire organization, from its leadership and staff to the products or services it delivers.

It did feel awkward using the now-banished term "brand" outside of the safety of the design department. MoMA's graphic designers have the benefit and pleasure of working in a place steeped in design history and populated by visually astute colleagues. Yet our work, if it's done well, should disappear and not call attention to itself. It was therefore no surprise when research showed a much higher public association with

Van Gogh's *Starry Night* and Picasso's *Les Demoiselles d'Avignon* than with the Museum's logo or typographic style. Without losing sight of our supporting role, we spent the next four years understanding the unique qualities of MoMA as it undertook the most ambitious building project in its history. Our branding process paralleled many of the steps prescribed within these pages, contributing to the smooth implementation of the Museum's new visual identity program.

When DK Holland first shared her online column at a resource site for nonprofits, I was certain it had the potential to be a great book. As with any other trade, designers can dissect a concept into abstraction when talking amongst themselves. DK makes these ideas accessible, tangible, and entertaining. It gives me great pleasure to know that she is using her many years of experience within the design community and directing it outwards. This publication brings together insights from some of the great visual communicators of our time, with DK as your friend and guide. Through these pages she will lead you through the entire process and show you the way to an authentic, successful, and sustainable brand—or whatever you choose to call it.

Ed Pusz, Director
Department of Graphic Design
The Museum of Modern Art

Branding for Nonprofits:

Developing Identity with Integrity

One

What's That Branding Buzz I Hear? And Why Nonprofits Can't Afford to Ignore It

> *Cowboys all know you can't brand nothin' till you tie three of its legs together, slam it to the ground, and sedate it.*
> *— Bart Crosby, brand designer*

Everything gets branded, one way or another—whether it's a consumer product, a movie star, a political cause, a religion . . . even a nonprofit organization. Branding can't be avoided, and, in fact, it should be embraced— by all nonprofits. After all, it's how you tell your story and it's at the heart of all outreach efforts.

Everyone wants to get attention. But the most organized, consistently delivered brands are the ones that people respond to. Why? Because they are the brands that communicate clearly to their audiences—and in response, people understand, know, and trust these brands.

Think about the nonprofit organizations that have gained your respect and interest. Can you sum up their brand message in a few simple words? Probably. For example:

- Public Broadcasting Service (*www.pbs.org*): The PBS logo—a simple black-and-white treatment of three faces in profile—conveys the graphic message that PBS puts people ahead of profits. And when you tune in to PBS, it looks and feels different from the networks in its use of images, color, format, typography. It has to—or it wouldn't be effectively branded.

Image 1. *The PBS logo*

- American Red Cross (*www.redcross.org*): An unadorned red cross against a field of white, the Red Cross logo is one of the most recognizable marks in the world. And the very qualities it conveys—neutrality, simplicity, and universality—are extremely important attributes of the organization's overall brand strategy. As the organization's tag line says, "Together, we can save a life." Simple, engaging, universal.

American Red Cross

Image 2. *The American Red Cross logo*

In both cases, design and branding work as respectful and effective partners. And, in both cases, the design is accessible, graphic, straightforward, memorable—a complement to the overall brand message of the organization.

The essential needs of the Red Cross included a logo that could alert people instantly—those in combat as well as distress—to the presence of the organization. Steff Geissbuhler, partner in Chermayeff & Geismar (*www.cgnyc.com*), a New York City design firm that has been among the most influential practitioners of non-profit identity design for nearly half a century, says, "The white Red Cross vehicles, flags, uniforms, and tents are extremely visible compared to the camouflage and battle fatigues of various armies." The logo, while exquisitely simple, is in fact a bit more complex in its meaning. Geissbuhler, who is Swiss, observes, "After World War II, Switzerland, a neutral country, was an appropriate location in which to negotiate and establish a multinational agreement designed to protect prisoners of war, which became known as the Geneva Convention. So the Red Cross logo was designed after the Swiss national symbol, but instead of a white cross on a red field, a red cross was placed on a white field. The white background represented hygiene and the red symbolized blood, and thus life."

The current PBS identity was designed by C&G partner Tom Geismar. When C&G designs a brand strategy, it doesn't just design a logo: It produces a manual that lays out meticulous guidelines for the use of various brand elements—logo, tag line, typefaces, formats, and color palette—and ensures the integrity of the system over time. "Each nonprofit really needs someone in a position of authority who understands design because good design establishes structure and meaning," says C&G partner Ivan Chermayeff, "while mediocre design leaves the viewer detached and uninspired." To make sure the brand strategy works in conjunction with the organization's identity, its administration is often elevated to an important staff function, with the overall strategy directed by a designated brand steward (typically, a senior executive). The nuts and bolts of that strategy are implemented on a day-to-day basis by staff and outside consultants, including designers and other communications professionals. The brand "team," in turn, is responsible for generating all the communications materials needed by the organization—including its annual report, brochures, letterhead, signage, the Web site, and so on—in a way that reinforces the brand.

In this book, I'll demystify the branding and design processes for nonprofits large and small and show you how you can use both to enhance the effectiveness of your organization. I'll talk to you about how brands are defined, as well as how to find and work with good designers and other professionals who understand branding and can help you create a brand strategy, within your budget, that supports the mission and identity of your organization. And, of course, I'll give you some ideas about where to find funding for all this.

This book is a handy reference full of case studies of well-branded nonprofits as well as practical, creative approaches to help you improve your brand and, in the process, become a more focused and effective organization.

Where Did This Branding Thing Come From?

At its most fundamental level, branding is driven by the human need to distinguish one thing from another. Think about all those old Westerns in which cows wandered onto some other rancher's range, causing all kinds of trouble: It was the rancher's brand that protected his herd—and his livelihood! On a more abstract, organizational level, the brand promotes the identity and underlying values of a unique culture by communicating the messages, products, and services created by that culture. For the purposes of our discussion, "brand strategy" is a plan that employs a unique set of design tools—logo, color palette, typefaces, formats, images, and language—created for an organization and applied in every communication vehicle that helps convey the brand identity: annual reports, letterhead, business cards, packaging, Web site, signage, and so on.

So brands are not just about logos (a typical misconception), even though the logo is often the key element in the branding program. The brand goes beyond tangible design elements to something more abstract and far-reaching. As an expression of the core values of your organization, your brand creates expectations and makes promises to your audiences—whether they're already captivated (staff, board members) or they're people you wish to attract (constituents, funders, opinion shapers). If executed well, a brand strategy delivers on those promises in a clear, understandable way that satisfies a need. In turn, brand loyalty—one of the keys to organizational sustainability—is earned by the consistent presentation of your brand and everything that your brand implies.

And Now, a Word from the Audience

Think of the brand as a play. And you are the audience. You stay with the plot when it is something you can relate to. You have empathy for the characters you understand and respect. You spread the word: This is a play to go see! Conversely, you walk out on a play that is confusing or ridiculous. And you tell all your friends *not* to go see it. If the playwright opens with another play, depending on your previous experience, you will or will not patronize it.

Similarly, a brand is talking to you, trying to gain your trust and loyalty—to get you to come back again and again. And if you, the audience, cannot respect this brand, it is quite often because the brand has failed to gain your understanding, and confidence. This is a brand that will not succeed. It's all about the audience.

The Branding Markers

Think of the things in your life that are branded—including yourself. All of these things exhibit, to a greater or lesser degree, aspects of the four branding markers:

▶ Reputation: How well is the brand known by its audiences?

▶ Esteem: How highly do its audiences rate the brand?

▶ Relevance: How much do the brand's audiences care about what it does or stands for?

▶ Differentiation: How different is the brand from others? Are other brands similar?

High marks in all four categories means the brand is probably strong and successful. But if you doubt that success is tied to these markers, just consider your own résumé: The higher you rank in these areas, the more impressive it will seem to potential employers—and conversely, the lower you rank, the less likely you are to succeed.

The nonprofit brand makes a promise to its audiences, which it usually incorporates into its mission statement—"To Serve the Most Vulnerable." The American Red Cross promises to remain neutral in providing relief to victims of disaster and to help people prevent, prepare for, and respond to emergencies in their communities. PBS promises to remain distanced from the commercial arena and, in the process, to deliver the best in broadcast news, entertainment, and education to its audiences.

Confident branding uses design to communicate a message that attracts the audiences you want, a message that creates confidence in your brand while differentiating what you offer—your product or service—from all others. Are you attracted to a product if you're unclear about what it does? Perhaps. It might be packaged in a sexy wrapper. Or it might be novel enough to pique your curiosity. But if the branding is flat, fuzzy, or fallacious, it probably won't sustain your interest, gain your trust—or earn your loyalty. The same holds true for nonprofit organizations.

Unfortunately, the nonprofit world is chock-full of fuzzy brands—mostly because nonprofit organizations are too busy focusing on service delivery or fundraising to consider the core work of branding. (Ironically, solid branding could help tremendously in these areas, as you'll see in the upcoming chapters.) Or, in the case of new organizations, they jump the gun and rush to pick a name or design a logo and prepare outreach materials, all the while neglecting the branding work that is vital to creating a sustainable identity. Adding insult to injury, they often do so without the benefit of guidance from a professional designer or marketer, or even input from their board. The result, more often than not, is branding that falls short: The organization's outreach materials don't end up communicating a clear and consistent message, or worse, the organization's story fails to resonate with its audiences, leaving the organization, if it manages to survive, struggling in catch-up mode.

It bears repeating: The benefits of an effective brand strategy, though not always immediately apparent, are substantial and, in the final analysis, well worth the time and resources required to realize them. Among other things, a solid branding program can:

▸ Communicate your organization's value proposition more efficiently and effectively.

▸ Grow the size of your audiences (including board members, clients, and potential funders and staff).

▸ Motivate your audiences to spread the word for you. And, of course, word of mouth is the best and cheapest form of advertising.

▸ Inform your next steps in terms of marketing and programming.

But maybe you don't know how to get started or are simply overwhelmed by the whole concept of branding. Don't worry. Help is on the way.

I've chosen two arts-related, New York City–based organizations to further explore the concept of branding—one a world-renowned cultural institution and the other a small, smart nonprofit that uses photography to explore the creativity of inner-city kids. Both have simple and effective brand identities. And they have one other thing in common: Art is the star of the show.

Make a Better Place, a storefront nonprofit on New York City's Lower East Side, has a big, important mission—to help New York City's public school kids express themselves through photography and creative writing projects. In doing so, they help these kids articulate a vision for change within their communities, as seen through their eyes.

Working with other nonprofit programs and the New York City Department of Education, Make a Better Place (or MABP, *www.makeabetterplace.org*) has, since 1994, helped many kids find their true voice and become chroniclers of their young lives and times. The results are moving and powerful. MABP has helped these kids advance their thinking. And the organization's branding is effective and subtle.

The Orchard Street storefront home of MABP is in the heart of the discount dry goods district of Manhattan. The sign on the building still says "Lolita Bras" (the prior tenant), but the bright and fresh photography visible through the plate-glass windows beckons passersby into the MABP gallery/workspace.

Inside MABP, Elana Gutmann, cofounder and director of MABP, says, "We chose Steve Liska, of Liska + Associates in Chicago, as our designer when we first started. Because he believes in photography, we knew he would honor the work of the kids and that his design and branding would be almost invisible. What kids see in our brochures is photography by kids just like themselves—communicating to them. And they see that their work is reproduced beautifully. They get excited because they see that they may be able to create work like this too, through MABP, and that their work may be published—and that also motivates them."

MABP still uses the exhibit signage system that Liska + Associates designed for them some years ago. It's simple, straightforward yet sophisticated, and confident in its use of color. The typography is elegant but understated. And it works just as well today as it did when Liska + Associates designed it because it's classic. Steve Liska, who is on MABP's board and is acknowledged in the organization's publications as a major sponsor, has always worked with MABP on a 100 percent pro bono basis. But the relationship is totally professional. Says Gutmann, "Steve doesn't just squeeze us in; he gives us the time and care we need. He's an angel—our angel."

Make A Better Place

Liska + Associates designed MABP's main brochure. The main image used in MABP's program materials is an extreme close-up of a wishing flower (dandelion). The photo, taken by Victor, age nine, who was separated from his mother, expresses his hope that they can be together again, perhaps living in a house like those seen in the background. It's a beautiful example of abstract thinking conveyed through imagery. Kids and teachers—two important audiences for MABP—see this and get the point that it's the kids' ideas—reflected in their photography and then elaborated on in their writing—that matters. Other audiences—funders and opinion shapers, for example—focus on two other things as well: great quality (signifying respect for the students' work) and professional execution. They are also likely to note that the organization is resourceful and valued, as reflected by the fact that the brochure's design was paid for by an Ideas That Matter grant from Sappi (*www.sappi.com*), an international paper company, a fact prominently noted in the publication.

The brochure is very successful, partly because the design is so visual. "We are an image-driven society," adds Gutmann. "We need to be able to communicate in a language that we can all understand. Kids experience how the images they see make them feel. It's not just chalk and talk. Our process engages multiple intelligences. Kids explore and learn about community, resources, and liabilities through reflection on their own experiences, research, community outings, and interviews with neighborhood residents. Later they are asked to create a variety of maps that may reflect physical topography, or kid-friendly environments, or areas of interest or danger. They learn to think abstractly, relating images to ideas. Within this active-learning environment, young people are able to demonstrate and communicate their understanding, their worldview, and their individuality. In this way, even those who may not have previously succeeded in traditional academic settings are provided the opportunity to shine." The new logo helps to convey this spirit—the frame featured in the organization's letterhead was developed when MABP shortened its name, originally called To Make the World a Better Place. Steve Liska told Gutmann and cofounder Daniele Robbiani that it was time for them to have a logo.

Designers Tanya Quick and Fernando Munoz, who had worked at Liska + Associates, were recruited. Gutmann and Robbiani articulated the mood and message they were trying to convey. Says Gutmann, "The concept of thinking of the possibilities—of thinking 'outside the box'—was a key value we wished to impart. The resulting logo has helped us expand the notion of 'frame' to include ideas like possibility and opportunity, without losing the reference to photography and the arts."

Image 5. The new MABP logo

Design is important in everything MABP does. Precise color and typographic choices are crucial because each element must enhance the kids' photography while combining to create a clear, simple organizational branding statement that doesn't overpower the work. It's a challenge not to over-design, to pull off a simple design in an elegant way. But MABP manages to do just that on a consistent basis across all media.

Web sites have become a major branding opportunity for organizations of all sizes. And yet Web design is just starting to reflect this fact—in part because the technology, in terms of design, was so limited for so long that designers simply weren't interested in the medium. As a result, most Web sites were places where everything was simply dumped on the home page, leaving visitors with a confusing impression of the organization. Now that the technology has improved and designers have more options and tools at their disposal, Web sites are starting to look more organized, strategic,

Image 6.
The MABP Web site

interesting—and branded. The MABP Web site (*www.makeabetterplace.org*) consistently uses the design elements featured in the organization's outreach materials, including logo, palette, typography, graphics, and images, all of which reinforce and strengthen the MABP brand. But while each page of the site is simple yet distinctive, the kids' photography is always the main focus.

MABP has not made outreach a main priority. But it has a good reputation and is held in high esteem in the New York educational community: Built on a well-branded and firm foundation, it's poised to grow, and as it does, it is positioned to further develop and exploit the design system it has had in place since its

Image 7. *Elana Gutmann (center front) surrounded by the staff of Make a Better Place*

inception. Nevertheless, its services could be imitated. The challenges for MABP going forward, therefore, are to spread the word about what it does, in a unique way, and convey the notion that no one could do it better or smarter. Branding and design will be key allies in that effort, because they are the prime ways that organizations can differentiate themselves from their competitors.

The Museum of Modern Art: Change As Opportunity

The Museum of Modern Art (*www.moma.org*), or MoMA, as it's affectionately known to art patrons around the world, was founded in 1929 by three women with eight prints and one drawing; in the decades since, it has grown to become arguably the most important museum of modern and contemporary art in the world. In order to maintain its position, however, MoMA (which is also called "the Modern") realized it needed to grow. Thus, when a building adjacent to its West 53rd Street Manhattan location became available in 1996, MoMA's trustees saw it as a unique opportunity to expand and improve its galleries—which had become inadequate for the display of large-scale contemporary art—while also enlarging its educational facilities.

But the plan posed a dilemma: What to do with MoMA's world-famous collections during the three years required to complete the expansion? And what about the MoMA design store and cinema, both of which were important educational components within the institution? Would the construction and attendant disruptions do more harm than good? Could MoMA weather three years of reduced visibility and the potential loss of significant amounts of earned income? These were real and serious concerns. But, at the same time, the trustees realized that the chance to expand in crowded midtown Manhattan was a once-in-a-generation opportunity and, moreover, brought with it the potential to not only significantly increase MoMA's influence in the world of modern art, but also strengthen its brand.

And so the decision was made to purchase the adjacent property and close the museum to allow for the proposed expansion. In the meantime, the 53rd Street collections were moved and new exhibitions were mounted in a temporary home in the borough of Queens; the new location was called MoMA QNS. The film center and its activities were moved to a small cinema in Manhattan. MoMA officials also decided to address the potential loss of revenue by

opening two new design stores (an important part of MoMA's revenue stream)—one at the temporary location in Queens and a second in Manhattan's gallery-rich Soho neighborhood—while keeping the original store on West 53rd Street open during the reconstruction period.

Branding—or re-branding—the institution, which already had a very distinct and focused identity, would be critical to the success or failure of the planned expansion of MoMA. Ed Pusz was the driving force behind the branding of MoMA QNS and has been MoMA's creative director since the capital campaign to fund the expansion of the 53rd Street location was launched in 1998. He says, "Prior to moving to Queens, we didn't need much branding. We had our logo, designed by

Chermayeff & Geismar in the 1960s, which was applied very straightforwardly on signage, letterhead, products, and brochures. So MoMA QNS was the first opportunity we had in a long time to say who we are and what we're becoming."

The MoMA QNS logo (design system by BaseDesign) was a key component of the distinctive and contemporary branded look when MoMA was in Queens. The simple typographic solution incorporates the abbreviation for "Queens" commonly used in New York's subways (QNS),

Image 10.
The MoMA QNS business card

and the famous MoMA acronym is rendered in a bold, direct typeface, creating a striking shape. "In its simplicity, the MoMA acronym transcends language," says Ruth Kaplan, the museum's deputy director for marketing and communications. "We find people recognize it merely by its shape." The bold simplicity of the logo allowed it to be manipulated and rendered in three dimensions without diminishing its integrity.

Ruth Kaplan adds, "We conduct surveys of our visitors constantly. So we knew well in advance that one big issue regarding our move would be the apprehension visitors had about traveling to Queens—about crossing the East River and not knowing what to expect once they were on the other side. Interestingly, this was much more of an issue for New Yorkers than it was for tourists. So the MoMA QNS branding was initially all about public transportation, movement, and change." MoMA could have shown ambivalence toward the relocation from chic West 53rd Street to a rough, raw industrial section of an outer borough but

Image 11.
MoMA has long been famous for selling branded products like this small notepad

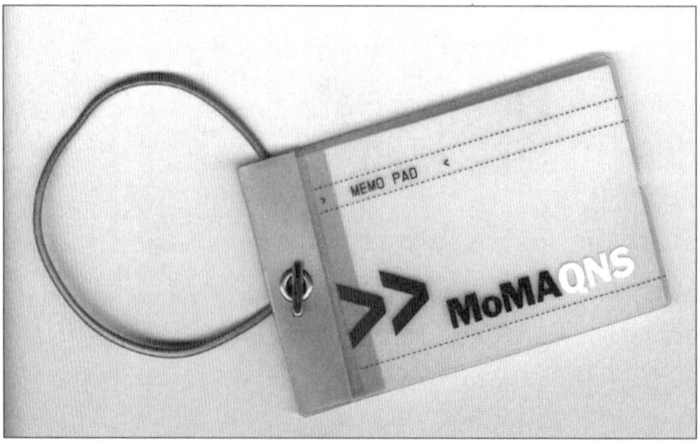

instead embraced the move to Queens with confidence, literally shouting it from the rooftops.

The Queens connection went back to 1999, when MoMA affiliated with P.S. 1, a very popular and successful contemporary arts center based in Queens since 1971. As part of the arrangement, the MoMA design team revised the logo for P.S. 1 (*www.ps1.org*) to incorporate the MoMA logo in an appropriately subordinate way, allowing the original P.S. 1 logo to remain the dominant element in the new design.

It's important to note that P.S. 1 officials had hired outside design consultants Lorraine Wilde and William Drenttel to evaluate the P.S. 1 brand, which led them to make these decisions. Meticulous planning is valued highly by MoMA.

Suggesting childlike inquisitiveness, P.S. 1 is housed in a nineteenth-century school building (all New York City public schools are numbered and start with "P.S.") and is located in Queens close to neighborhoods like Long Island City and Astoria, and Fort Greene, Williamsburg, and Greenpoint in Brooklyn, all of which have become popular with artists in recent years.

Image 12. *The P.S. 1 incorporated the MoMA logo in an appropriately subordinate way. Auspiciously, the logos were in harmony prior to the merger.* Design: 2X4, Inc.

Image 13.
P.S. 1 is housed in a nineteenth-century school building. Logo design: 2X4, Inc.

The results of the move to Queens, not surprisingly, were astounding for MoMA. "Matisse-Picasso," the second major show at MoMA QNS in its second year, was a huge success and sold out regularly. Shuttle

buses carried museum-goers from West 53rd Street to MoMA QNS's front door and also made the hop to P.S. 1, just ten minutes away.

Cafés and gift shops at both MoMA venues provide sustenance, branded mementos, and income for the museum. The re-branding campaign also increased interest in the museum through its new locations. The unconventional and, in some cases, daring decisions made by the MoMA team have modernized the brand a bit, making it seem more relevant to the times while enhancing its reputation as the leading institution in the field of contemporary art. Part of that relevance is expressed in the presence that MoMA now has on the Web.

Image 14. *The MoMA Web site. Design: Allegra Burnette and the Department of Digital Media at the Museum of Modern Art*

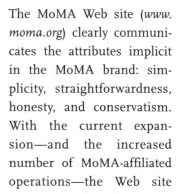

The MoMA Web site (*www. moma.org*) clearly communicates the attributes implicit in the MoMA brand: simplicity, straightforwardness, honesty, and conservatism. With the current expansion—and the increased number of MoMA-affiliated operations—the Web site became even more important to the brand, weaving its many components together in a way that suggests the sum is greater than the parts.

Image 15. *MoMA moved back to Manhattan in 2005 right on schedule, closing down its temporary public exhibition space in Queens, retrofitting it for other purposes*

The architecture of the new MoMA (designed by Yoshio Taniguchi) surprised many: It is not the most modern-looking building in Manhattan. But that reflects the MoMA brand brilliantly—MoMA's about the art, not the architecture.

MoMA's main challenge going forward is to maintain its relevance—and its dynamic identity—now that it has returned to its 53rd Street location with thunderous applause and record-breaking attendance. It's exciting to anticipate what the MoMA design team will come up with next—and that may be the greatest compliment a brand can receive.

Image 16. *The Museum of Modern Art, designed by Yoshio Taniguchi. Entrance at 53rd Street.* © 2004 Timothy Hursley

Image 17. *The Museum of Modern Art's Department of Graphic Design in the Abby Aldrich Rockefeller Sculpture Garden at the Museum of Modern Art. Back row, left to right: Ingrid Chou, Kate Johnson, Bonnie Ralston, Junghee Hahm, James Kuo. Front row, left to right: Ed Pusz, Elan Cole, Melanie Malkin, Althea Penza, Burns Magruder, Claire Corey.* Photo: 2005 James Kuo

Two

Anatomy of a Design Brief: Start to Get Your Nonprofit Brand in Focus

It's human nature for people to identify with the celebrities they see and read and hear about in the media. In fact, they often develop loyalties to celebrities based on what they know, or think they know, about the perceived values and belief systems of those celebrities. Celebrities able to project an image that seems direct, consistent, admirable, and authentic—think Hillary Clinton, Bono, or the Dalai Lama—usually have a more loyal following than celebrities who are perceived to be wishy-washy or phony. In the same sense, in order to be effective, branding has to have clarity and depth.

Just like the effective celebrity brand, your organization's brand has to convey the key values of your organization—values rooted in its core activities—if you hope to develop a loyal following. And that's why it's important that you, your board, and your colleagues—the people who, day in and day out, work to make your nonprofit a success—are involved in and committed to the branding process, starting with the creation of a design brief.

As a distillation of your organization's mission, values, and personality, the design brief is an essential tool that, with a little luck and a lot of hard work, will lead to the development of a brand that effectively conveys what your organization does and stands for.

There's no question that the board has to sign off on the organization's branding. But first, the board needs to have a clear handle on the mission and vision of the organization in order to be able to give direction.
– Carolyn Patterson, President Emeritus
of Governance Matters

Unfortunately, many nonprofits are too quick to hand the organization's branding over to an outside consultant and assume a reactive rather than proactive approach to the process. Worse than that, many consultants who work with nonprofits skip the development of a design brief altogether. How can consultants possibly tell your story without you? The answer is they can't—and trying to do so often leads to unwelcome consequences, not the least of which is the possibility that your organization will have to live with an ineffective, half-baked brand.

While having a design brief is no guarantee that your nonprofit can avoid that fate, a thorough, well-constructed brief can go a long way toward providing a solid foundation for the construction of your brand and will ensure that you and your outside consultants are on the same page at the start of the process.

You start by providing the creative team with the information they need to help you tell your story.

Outlining the Design Brief

When you sit down to develop a design brief, be sure to consider the following:

1. **Profile:** What does your organization do? And why does it matter? Be as succinct as possible and be sure to work your mission and values statements into your response.

2. **Context:** What is happening in the world today that makes your mission relevant and compelling to your target audiences?

3. **Positioning:** What is your organization's relationship with others that are similar in size and mission? Be sure to include your competitors' logos and Web site URLs so that you can start to see how those organizations fit into your universe, and vice versa.

4. **Audiences:** List your audiences, starting with your primary audience (e.g., constituents) and continuing through secondary and tertiary audiences (funders, board, etc). Now ask yourself the following: Whom are we trying to reach that we haven't already? What do our audiences value that we already provide, or could provide? Do we have any research or demographic information about our audiences that we can share with the creative team?

5. **Brand personality:** How would you describe your organization's personality? How does the community view your organization? Are you perceived favorably? Are you seen as active and involved, or as distant and aloof? Are you a young organization or well established? (If you don't know the answers to these questions, you may have to do some research.)

6. **Current situation:** What aspect(s) of your current situation precipitated the need for a new or revised brand strategy?

7. **Budget:** How much are you willing to spend? Yes, it's hard to formulate a budget when you don't know what the solution is, but you should find a way to give the creative team an idea of how much you are

willing/able to invest in the process. For instance, tell the designers the size of your staff and how much you rely on volunteer efforts. If they can't afford to work pro bono, they have to charge according to what they must make on the project while calculating a non-profit discount into their fee, if appropriate.

8. **Schedule/deadlines:** What is the time frame for the project? Are there deadlines that absolutely must be met (e.g., the date of a specific event or anniversary)?

9. **Design media:** What kind of materials are you going to need? A basic brochure? An annual report? A Web site? Letterhead, cards, envelopes? Posters or signage? A PowerPoint presentation or multimedia piece?

10. **Technical/practical requirements:** Are there specific requirements that must be spelled out in advance of the design process? For instance, is your organization required to use union labor? How about environmentally friendly resources such as recycled paper or soy inks? Dual computer platforms for templates (Mac and PC)? You'll want to make a note in the brief if that's the case.

The Branding Markers

To review, the four markers are reputation (How well known is your organization?); esteem (How highly thought of is your organization?); relevance (How important are your organization's mission and activities to the concerns of your target audiences?); and differentiation (Are there other organizations out there that do what your organization does? Is your organization distinct from those other organizations in the minds of your target audiences?).

The branding markers should be included in every nonprofit organization's toolkit. To see why, draw a simple L-shaped chart, with the four markers arrayed along the vertical axis and the numbers 1 to 10 spaced along the horizontal axis. Now ask yourself: How valued is your organization by your audience? If you have reason to believe that 50 percent of the audience knows of your organization, put an X above the 5 next to "reputation." If your organization is totally unique and therefore has no competition (good for you!), give yourself a 10 next to "differentiation," and so on until you've graded all four markers.

Identifying your weaker markers lets you know what you need to work on, while the stronger ones tell you what you can count on. Strong brands can have weak markers, but some are of more concern than others. For instance, if your brand is unique and well respected but irrelevant to your primary audience, you have a major problem. If, on the other hand, your brand is highly relevant and well respected but not particularly well known, you still have a problem, but it's one that can more easily be rectified.

That's why it's important for the creative team to know at the beginning of the design process just what your brand strengths and weaknesses are—so that the team can play to your strengths while minimizing your weaknesses.

Branding by Committee

Now that you're familiar with the basic elements of the design brief, the next step is to make sure that your organization's executive director and senior staff—working with outside consultants as needed—are involved in developing the brief. And once the brief has been completed, present it to your board for review.

Carolyn Patterson, president emeritus of Governance Matters, says, "There's no question that the board has to sign off on the organization's branding. But first, the board needs to have a clear handle on the mission and vision of the organization in order to be able to give direction."

Now, you may be thinking that your board members are either uninterested in or incapable of thinking about design issues and branding strategies. In which case, I'd suggest that when it comes to issues of design and branding, board members can only be effective if they understand these issues in context. And that's one important purpose of the design brief. Let me tell you a story.

Beth Fredrick, vice president of communications and development at the Alan Guttmacher Institute in New York City, and two of her colleagues visited me a while back with a problem: Most of the Institute's publications (of which there are many) looked nothing alike. As Fredrick noted, "Each publication targets a different audience and serves a different purpose. But on the other hand, no one ever sees all of them together. Is there a better way to unify them and promote an image for the Institute?"

She was right. Although her organization's publications derived from the same institutional culture, some were bold and modern in appearance, while others were quite subdued and scholarly—and there wasn't any connection between the different looks and designs. Without a unifying theme, the publications tended to blur the unique attributes of the Guttmacher Institute and, in terms of branding, cancel each other out. What Beth and her colleagues needed, I suggested, was an institutional dialog that included the mission statement and focused on developing a design brief to use as a springboard for a coherent brand strategy.

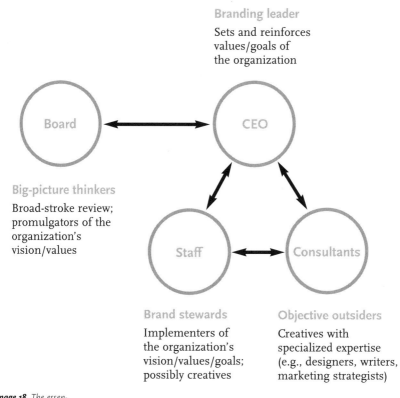

Branding leader
Sets and reinforces
values/goals of
the organization

Board

CEO

Big-picture thinkers
Broad-stroke review;
promulgators of the
organization's
vision/values

Staff

Consultants

Brand stewards
Implementers of
the organization's
vision/values/goals;
possibly creatives

Objective outsiders
Creatives with
specialized expertise
(e.g., designers, writers,
marketing strategists)

Image 18. *The essential roles of the branding team*

Beth told me that 1) she and her colleagues were about to welcome a new brand-savvy CEO into the fold and this was an ideal opportunity to start talking about the brand, 2) the process should involve senior staff and the board, and 3) the brief should include the purpose of each publication and a description of how it related to the overall brand. The latter would serve to focus all the stakeholders, including the board and senior staff, on the task at hand. As Beth later observed, "The tough part is where the directive comes from. Everyone involved with your organization needs a branding mentality; otherwise it's a real challenge to use design in strategic and effective ways. That directive comes from the top."

Beth understood that every organization, regardless of size, has to grapple with its own branding conundrums sooner or later. Nonprofits that are able to provide a design brief to their creative teams and bring key staff and board members into the process have a better chance of getting on the right road—the road to an effective brand—than organizations that try to get there without a map or the participation of key stakeholders.

There are exceptions, of course, and the fact that some organizations succeed in branding themselves effectively without a design brief or buy-in from the board should not be taken as an argument for adopting the by-the-seat-of-your-pants approach to branding. As often as not, their success is attributable to the special talents of one or two people and more than a little luck. With that in mind, here's a tiny nonprofit that has been able to leverage the mighty talents of its founders into a strong and effective brand.

PUPS: Sniffing Out the Brand

Fort Greene Park Users and Pets Society (PUPS), a volunteer-run membership organization in the Fort Greene neighborhood of Brooklyn, is so new and small that it still hasn't received its determination letter from the IRS. It has a tiny board and not much funding. Yet it has gotten off to a beautiful start, branding-wise.

Image 19. The PUPS logo shows a paw print under a tree, representing the twin concerns of the organization: the dogs and the park in Fort Greene, Brooklyn

In terms of expressing its core values and implementing its brand strategy, its strengths include:

▶ The PUPS mission statement is straightforward and establishes the unique positioning of the organization: "We are responsible dog owners who believe that in order to enjoy the park's beautiful grounds and many resources, we must clean up after our dogs, keep our dogs under control, and prevent our dogs from harming the park's landscape."

▶ The organization's audiences are easily defined. Its primary audience, numbering in the hundreds, is anyone who walks his or her dog(s) in Fort Greene Park. Secondary audiences include: New York City Parks Department officials and employees, residents of Fort Greene who use the park but don't have dogs, and neighborhood associations.

▶ The organization regularly surveys its members and incorporates many of the comments/ideas generated by those surveys into its activities and materials to make sure it remains relevant and responsive to its members while aware of the needs of the other audiences as well.

▶ The acronym form of the organization's name, PUPS, is short, clever, relevant, and easy to remember—all qualities that reinforce the brand. Plus it has a touch of whimsy, which is also entirely appropriate, since having fun is one of the key values espoused by the organization.

Image 20. The covers of the official PUPS calendars reflect the core values of the PUPS brand—the love and caring for dogs and Fort Greene Park

▶ The organization has no competition, so it's highly differentiated in the minds of its target audiences.

▶ The PUPS Web site (*www.fortgreenepups.org*) is bright, well designed, and chock-full of valuable resources for members. Even better, the organization presents clearly defined short- and long-term goals right on the site and informs visitors to the site when a goal has been reached. Brightly colored links draw your eye to the organization's many activities.

▶ The organization has good marketing instincts. Its products—T-shirts and a calendar—resonate with the organization's target audiences and reinforce its brand while generating revenue. People are never featured—only implied—in the calendar, and rarely on the Web site. This keeps

the focus on the pups. People rave about this calendar—it's a hot seller. One member sent a copy to a friend in New Jersey, who clamored for more, saying, "You actually know these dogs?" as if they were celebrities!

Image 21. From left: The 2005 board of PUPS: Nancy Peterson, Secretary (with Charley and Tim), Amy Hecht, Vice President (with Bingo and Carly), and Kath Hansen, President (with Cameron). The humans are all wearing PUPS T-shirts designed by Hecht. Photo: 2005 Michelle Fornof

Surprise, surprise! Up until recently, PUPS was run by just two people—a graphic designer named Amy Hecht and Kath Hansen, a marketing professional (with a lot of support from Amy's accounting-savvy husband, Maurice van Swaaij). Together, Hecht and Hansen developed the PUPS brand, including its mission/values statements, logo, Web site, and income-generating products. But it's precisely because PUPS is small, coupled with the fact that Hecht and Hansen are design/ marketing professionals, that the

organization was able to develop a strong brand in a cost-effective manner without benefit of a written design brief: It was all in their very professional heads.

Image 22. The PUPS logo is rendered in black and white—but in a sophisticated way—on the PUPS Web site (www. fortgreenepups.org), next to an array of brightly colored links. Web site design: Amy Hecht, Brown Stone Studio

Thanks in part to its effective branding, PUPS members "get" the organization and show up in large numbers for events. And because they're able to describe what it does in simple, easy-to-understand language, they also tend to be excellent word-of-mouth promoters of its value to the community. Recently, when Hecht and Hansen realized they needed to expand the organization's leadership ranks, they put out a call for others to get involved, and were pleasantly surprised when dozens of members (including excellent design and photography professionals) volunteered. And with all sorts of new plans on the PUPS drawing board, Hecht, Hansen, and their colleagues are already at work on a formal design brief that will be used to guide the organization's future expansion.

So now you too should be on your way to developing a design brief, to getting your CEO and senior managers to think about branding issues, and to securing the best wishes of your board.

Three

It Takes a Village to Raise a Brand: The Roles and Responsibilities of the Branding Team

 Building consensus is essential to the success of the branding process.

In the last chapter, I talked about the importance of conducting research at the beginning of the design process. I outlined what goes into a design brief, and talked about getting everyone onto the same branding page. By now, I'm sure you're wondering who is responsible for pulling all this together.

Early on in the branding process, an individual (or two) may stand out as having the necessary authority, instincts, and drive to develop the brand. That person (or group of people) must come from within your organization. It could be your executive director or another high-level staff person and/or board member. But regardless of who it is, this person (or group of people) should possess the following:

▶ Visual/verbal acuity

▶ A facility for abstract thinking

▶ An organized but flexible management style

- ▸ The ability to work effectively as part of a group

- ▸ The respect of his or her peers

Once this individual (or group) is chosen, he or she should be designated the brand steward(s). The brand steward's job is to take the raw information gathered in the initial research phase (see the previous chapter for a more complete description of that process) and, from it, assemble the formal design brief. While all design briefs are different, the good ones manage to provide context for the brand, clarify the need for a new or revamped brand to the team and to the designer, set forth goals for the branding process, and rally the troops around the effort.

This last point cannot be overstated: Building consensus is essential to the success of the branding process. Everyone with a stake in the brand—your board members, staff, funders, constituents, consultants, opinion-shapers—should feel that his or her views and concerns are captured in the design brief. The reason is simple: It facilitates buy-in and enhances the credibility of the process, resulting in a richer, more potent brand. Thus, the first responsibility of good brand stewardship is to make sure that the final design brief is inclusive and gets the ball rolling in the right direction.

The Long and Short of It

As I've mentioned, every design brief is uniquely structured, and their lengths vary wildly. The Museum of Modern Art (MoMA) prepared several briefs for its expansion, and although the strategy it settled on was bold and courageous (and its briefs were far from brief), the process it engaged in is a good model for any nonprofit considering a major brand overhaul.

Ed Pusz, director of design at MoMA and one of its brand stewards, recalls the museum's efforts to create a design brief informed by consensus. "We held a series of debates about the future of the museum. The brief we used for architects was based largely on these discussions. And we've written several briefs since then for other parts of the strategy. The brief is an invaluable tool for the design process. It's so easy for people to get caught up in what they like and don't like. But when you have a brief, you can always refer back to the ideas that were agreed to in it."

One thing the brief should not do is to dictate the design of the organization's visual identity. Instead, it should relate informative facts and substantiated opinions about the organization's current identity and/or ideas about the overall identity. For instance, MoMA's brief included a six-page executive summary that outlined the museum's history, its place within the global arts community, its mission and commitment to that mission, the goals for its expansion, and, in brutally honest language, the challenges it faced going forward. The goal was, and should be, to get everything out on the table and agreed to in writing. Because design ultimately involves making a lot of subjective decisions (regarding color, typography, form, etc.), the design brief helps to protect against irrationality creeping into and possibly ruining the process. If you're able to point back to something that was stated in the brief, you have a better chance of short-circuiting the person who says, "We can't use red. I really hate red." As Pusz notes, "It only takes one person to derail the branding process. The brief keeps the train on the tracks." (For examples of MoMA's current branding strategy, refer back to chapter 1.)

Of course, not every nonprofit organization will want or have the resources to create a detailed design brief with a six-page executive summary. In many cases, a free-ranging conversation involving the various stakeholders and using information gleaned from the initial research phase may be enough. But however you decide to approach it, a decision should be made early on about how much unity is required to keep the process moving forward. Which audiences need to buy into the brand strategy? The staff? The board? Your funders? The answer to this question should tell you what it will take to secure consensus.

The Ultimate Design Challenge: Designing for Designers

Bart Crosby at Bart Crosby Associates (*www.crosbyassociates.com*), an AIGA fellow and a revered

brand graphic designer, developed the AIGA brand a few years ago—a mammoth and daunting challenge, since the AIGA, with forty-six chapters and 15,000 members, is the established national organization for graphic designers.

Crosby was chosen to lead the branding process because of his evenhanded dedication to the organization's principles and his excellent reputation as a brand

Image 23.
Bart Crosby

designer. One of his first steps was to develop "Branding the AIGA," a simply designed document that laid out the situation and explained what branding was all

about and why it was important for the AIGA to be branded. (See appendix B) This was circulated to the organization's entire membership, including several accomplished graphic designers who had been selected to consult with him as he developed the brand.

Once the re-branding strategy was complete, Crosby produced a branding manual

Image 24. *The AIGA branding manual*

to show how to apply the AIGA logo in a branded yet flexible way. Note that the new logotype is neatly contained in a fixed position inside a box. The manual is titled, appropriately, "Thinking Inside the Box." It was also distributed to the entire membership and to anyone working on any projects that involved creating branded materials for the AIGA.

"Branding the AIGA" functioned somewhat like a brief. It started with an explanation of branding that included an extensive section called "Is Our Logo Our Brand?" His conclusion: Yes and no. The AIGA logo was an important component of the organization's brand because, as Crosby put it, it was the "identifier." In the case of AIGA, it's a way to identify a product— and they have many—as theirs. For instance, each publication is produced by a different designer and together they reflect the full spectrum of the AIGA's design roster and talent. The AIGA logo is applied to each one, and as such becomes the common element that ties them all together—i.e., the brand identifier.

You have to look closely at these pages from Crosby's brand manual to see the genius behind his system. It's subtle. The AIGA logotype (originally designed in the 1960s by the legendary designer Paul Rand) was modified by Crosby. By placing the logo inside a box, the logo allows for greater versatility in application. If you look closely, you can see a number of differently sized logos, in multiple relationships, on the page. The texture and color of the box can change, and it can even be put on a jaunty angle when appropriate. Without the box device, the logo floated in space, leading to design problems in many situations and weakening the logo's readability significantly. Because

Image 25.
A page from the AIGA brand manual designed by Bart Crosby

many different designers create posters, signage, and publications for the organization, each in his or her style, the flexibility provided by the device is critical to the logo's usefulness. Crosby's manual serves to both inform and empower both the organization and the individual designers who will put the brand into use.

The fact that Crosby, in his brief, spent a significant amount of time educating graphic designers on the subject of branding is also something to consider when preparing yours. If nothing else, it is a reminder that designers are not universally well versed in this area, and is something to consider when you get to the point of interviewing designers, many of whom will say they are involved in branding but do little more than design logos.

Crosby also included a section in the brief called "How Do We Do It?" which spoke to all AIGA members as potential branding partners—not just as designers, but as writers, creators of products and services, editors, proofreaders—and held them "personally responsible for ensuring that the attributes of the organization are embodied in every effort." Then he pointed out that this could not be achieved through the production of a guide or manual—it required a deeper understanding of the brand by all participants.

The 800-Pound Albatross

There is one more aspect of branding that is crucial to consider at this juncture: naming. Does your organization have the correct name? Has your name been converted into an acronym that makes sense and is useful? Do you have a name that has been reduced to a meaningless "initialism"—an abbreviation formed only from the initial letter of constituent words and pronounced as the individual letters—e.g., ACLU (American Civil Liberties Union) or IBM (for International Business Machines)? For the vast number of established organizations, naming

is a done deal. Some of you, I'm sure, are absolutely hor-
rified at the very idea of reconsidering your name. That's
understandable. But you aren't doing yourself any favors
by ignoring it if it's a big problem. An out-of-date, inap-
propriate, or just plain clunky name can be like an 800-
pound albatross around your organization's neck.

Because they usually start out small and with limited
resources, nonprofits often name themselves in haste
without any professional help. Again, there is a reason:
They're focused on a cause, not on a marketing scheme.
But their organization may have to live with the detri-
mental effects of a bad naming decision for the rest of its
life (or until they and their colleagues bite the bullet and
change the name, whichever comes first). Don't make that
mistake. Turn the situation around before it's too late.

When founded in 1914, AIGA stood for American Institute of
Graphic Arts. AIGA no longer uses the full name because the
term graphic arts *no longer relates to the core membership.*
Yet AIGA feels there is too much equity in its name to change
it so it remains simply AIGA—a rather meaningless ini-
tialism—to anyone at the periphery of the design profession.

I suggest that you conduct a modest amount of research if
there is any question at all about the meaning and/or value
of your organization's name. To start, make a short list of
individuals you trust who also represent your various audi-
ences and ask them, individually and privately, the following:

▶ *What does the organization's name mean to you? Parse*
the words if that helps.

▶ *Is the name confusing or otherwise hindering your mission?*

▶ *If you use an acronym or initialism in your collateral*
materials, is its meaning clear and unambiguous, or does
it confuse or otherwise harm the brand?

▶ *Do you have a tagline? If so, does it clarify your mission*
and serve to motivate your constituents, or is its meaning
fuzzy or off base?

The answer may be, as with the AIGA, that the name must stay, but you will have come to the conclusion the right way—through methodical research.

In the first chapter, I told the story of an organization called Make a Better Place, which was originally called To Make the World a Better Place. After several years of answering the phone that way (a form of torture), the founders decided to shorten the name, and the payoff was almost immediate. People could remember the new name, the directors weren't tongue-tied every time they had to talk about the organization, and they got a shorter initialism out of it that they could actually use internally and in conversation. (Just try to work "TMWBP" into a conversation!) Although this was not ideal (since MABP is not a word), it was a logical compromise: To Make the World a Better Place was too well known at this point to change to a completely new name.

Know Your Nomenclature

As part of the branding process, the brand team and designer will create a vocabulary to describe your organization and its programs and activities. This is called "nomenclature," and in addition to your organization's name, it includes taglines, acronyms, titles, and phrases that are particular to your organization; they are a reflection of your cause and your culture.

As part of its recent re-branding, for example, AIGA decided to create programs and publications that featured one or two short words. Thus, the association's business publication was relaunched as Gain: AIGA Journal of Designing Business, *its annual was renamed* 365: AIGA Year in Design, *and the association's online publication was called* Voice: AIGA Journal of Design, *in addition to conferences called* Gain *and* Move. *This use of one word creates brand continuity.*

An organization with a long, complicated name will usually create a shorter version of the name, either an acronym—a pronounceable word such as PUPS (short for

Park Users and Pets Society) or MADD (Mothers Against Drunk Driving) formed from the initial letters of the constituent words—or an initialism. Quite often, these shorter versions become the name most commonly used when referring to an organization.

There is a hybrid—the initialism that creates a new word, like NATO (North Atlantic Treaty Organization) or UNICEF (United Nations International Children's Fund). The bigger nonprofit organizations (or NPOs) are not hard to remember, but initialisms of smaller NPOs can be mind-boggling. Without a doubt, the Guinness World Record for initialisms goes to TDCTJHTBIPCU—The Design Conference That Just Happens to Be in Park City, Utah—an annual event that has been held for more than twenty years. Obviously the initialism here is a parody and, because of that, it works. However, since initialisms, in general, are just a convenience that communicates nothing, they can take over and the branding can run amuck. Know any organizations using initialisms that don't even tell you what they stand for? Maddening. Either they assume you know, or what it stands for is no longer what they stand for. Either way, the initials are not adding to the branding effort.

Naming is complicated and should be approached perspicaciously. Most organizations—large, established organizations at that—have talked to me about the frustration of dealing with their names. In one case, the organization's acronym meant exactly what the organization was working against, while in another instance, the organization had been named in 1960 for an area of town that no longer existed. A third's name is very close to that of another, larger organization based in the same city. All were relatively successful regardless, but they also knew that their names were holding them back. Unfortunately, of these three organizations, two understandably did not relish the idea of re-branding their organizations with a new name, and to this day neither has taken any action to *change. The third, a far younger organization, successfully made the change.*

When the brand steward(s) is confident he or she has created the best design brief he or she can, and it has been approved, it's time to circulate it to designers and others who may be called upon to help your organization in the design development phase. I can't stress strongly enough how the brief paves the way to a creative process that is infused with enthusiasm and confidence, and helps ensure a positive outcome.

"Good communication is intentional," notes Aaron Hurst, founder and president of the Taproot Foundation (*www.taprootfoundation.org*), a nonprofit organization with offices in San Francisco and New York that pairs qualified nonprofits with volunteer designers. "In a successful design project, you need to develop a thoughtful brief that articulates a focused and commonly held set of goals for the project that can be used by the design team to keep its efforts headed in the right direction. Without such a brief, there is a risk that the effort will fail." And since success is your ultimate goal, remember that, no matter how impatient others get, it's good for you to take the time you need in this phase to get it right.

Four

Getting the Team Ready to Birth the Brand

In the last chapter, I suggested that it's essential to honor the evolution of the design process. Skip a sequence and the process can drive right off a cliff. That's why it's important, before you get started, to make sure the members of your design team are familiar with the various stages of—and roles they'll be expected to play in—the process.

Phase One: Research and Orientation

There is no single answer to the question "Who should be on the branding team?" For most organizations, the primary consideration is the availability of resources. If money is tight and you already have two or three people on staff or on your board with the vision, talent, and tools needed to develop a robust brand, then that's how many people you should have on your team. Some organizations may not be so lucky; as a rule, people tend to be limited in their design expertise and often have somewhat sketchy views about design and what constitutes an effective brand. Besides, when it comes to something as important as your brand, which has to speak to multiple audiences with different needs and expectations, it's healthy to have a range of personalities, abilities, sensibilities and viewpoints represented on the team—as long as the individuals in question are educated about branding (i.e., they've read this book) and can get along.

In my experience, the most effective branding teams have around five to seven members. Not coincidentally, there happen to be five distinct roles on the team (see the diagram in chapter 2). They are:

- Brand leader

- Brand steward(s)

- Board representative

- Writer

- Graphic designer

The brand leader, usually your CEO or executive director, is the articulator and champion of your organization's vision and values. He or she monitors the branding process to make sure the brand strategy remains true to the core vision and values.

The brand steward(s), usually a ranking member of your management team, makes sure that all applications of the brand are executed well and keeps the brand strategy on target on a day-to-day basis. During the development phase, the steward also calls the meetings, sets the agenda, and keeps the design process on track.

The board representative makes sure the concerns of the board are accurately reflected in the brand strategy and reports back to the board as progress is made. In exceptional circumstances (e.g., when no board member is able and/or willing to serve on the branding team), this function may be filled by the brand leader. I recommend, however, that you recruit someone with branding expertise to your board.

Whether a professional or staff person who writes well, the writer's job is to help develop the brand using words and concepts that complement the look and feel, or "trade dress" (typography, color palette, imagery, logo, etc.), created by the designer. Trade dress refers to the constants that define the brand identity. The words and images must work together to create a cohesive "voice" for your brand, and that voice has to be authentic and have depth in order for the brand to resonate. In my experience, it is often difficult for an outside person to pull this off unless he or she has had a long relationship with the organization in question. Chapter 10 talks about developing staff to take on the writing function, and you may want to jump ahead at this point.

With the exception of the brand leader, the graphic designer is the most critical person on the branding team: It's his or her job to bring the emotional (i.e., visual) component of the brand to life. Whether someone on staff or an outside consultant, the designer has to "get it"; if he or she doesn't, your design process is in trouble—and no amount of discussion is likely to save it. If you do decide to hire an outside design consultant, you may choose to assemble the rest of the team first so that every team member can be involved in the decision. Doing so will boost morale by showing the team it has control of the process, and help ensure that the team has confidence in the designer you choose (and confidence is highly contagious).

Style and Strategy

Before you choose a designer, you may want to spend some time—alone and as a group—developing an awareness of design styles and brand strategies in the broadest sense. You can start by talking about the brands you love or hate, focusing on why they work or miss the mark. To get an idea of the kind of work that's being done, you might also want to look at graphic design annuals such as those published by *Communication Arts* (*www.commarts.com*), the premier publication in the graphic design field; *PRINT* magazine (*www.printmag.com*), publisher of the Regional Design Annual; AIGA (*www.aiga.org*), the largest organization for

graphic design professionals in the United States; and *Graphis* (*www. graphis.com*), an important international design publication. Most of these publications are available at libraries, good newsstands, and bookstores, or through their Web sites; AIGA and *Communications Arts* even offer search-

Image 26. PRINT
magazine Web site

able databases of designers on their sites. Remember, if you see a designer whose work appeals to you, be sure to share your discovery with other members of the team so that all members have an opportunity to develop a keener awareness of design, as well as each other's likes and dislikes.

Image 27. Graphis
magazine Web site

Image 28. *AIGA Web site design: Flat Inc.*

Image 29. Communication Arts *magazine Web site*

The next step is to conduct an internal brand audit. The audit should include an accounting of all the "tools" used to build your brand: brochures, letter-head, program literature, newsletters, annual reports, Web pages, marketing materials, signage, uniforms—anything related to your organization's current, as well as future, visual identity. Make a chart and note how successful each of these has been in promoting your brand. Be sure to write down the purpose of the piece, its importance, and its priority in terms of the organizational scheme of things. Don't worry if, during the audit, you discover that you have three brochures where one would suffice or marketing materials that work at cross-purposes with your fundraising appeals. The purpose of the audit is to expose exactly these kinds of redundancies and inconsistencies, while "mapping" all current applications of your brand and generating ideas for the design process that is about to unfold.

Last, but not least, determine which organizations you compete against, as well as other organizations in your universe, and divide the list among members of the team. Have them research the organizations on their list, identifying brand elements that work or fall flat. Make sure you consider a representative sampling of branded materials—logo treatments, advertisements, Web pages, etc.—for each organization, and be sure to include some physical objects—annual reports, business cards, brochures, and so on. Pay particular attention to how other organizations have solved branding problems you may be facing, as well as problems that seem to defy solution. And don't forget to see if you can identify the "promise"—the fundamental message—inherent in each brand. Knowledge of how these other organizations have resolved their identity issues will help you do better—to differentiate yours from theirs.

After you've completed your research, compare your notes with those of other members of the team and, for each organization, ask yourselves the following:

▶ Is the brand's "voice" convincing? Consistent?

▶ Is the brand true to the organization's vision and values?

▶ Can you articulate the "promise" inherent in each brand?

▶ Is the brand trying to appeal to a primary audience? If so, who is it?

This is one of those rare occasions when what matters is what you can casually observe: If you don't "get" what a brand is trying to convey just by looking at it, then the chances are good that the brand or its strategy is flawed.

After you've gone through this process for a number of organizations, take a careful look at your own brand, compare it to the others, and ask yourselves the following:

▶ What is our brand promise?

▶ Does it appeal to our primary audience?

▶ Does our current identity undervalue our brand?

▶ Does our current identity undermine our brand?

▶ What are we doing well/poorly in terms of branding?

▶ How do we want to position our brand so that it's more effective?

Design is planning. All of these exercises will prepare you and your branding teammates to actively participate in the birth of your brand. As designer Bart

Crosby says, "The brand is a living thing." It's up to the branding team to develop a brand with a heartbeat. But the brand also has to have sufficient depth and breadth to allow it to grow and adapt to changing circumstances. And circumstances will change— that's about the only thing you can count on.

Five

Spotlight on Designers: What They Do and How They Do It

In the previous chapter, I talked about the various roles members of the branding team play and I stressed the importance that discernment plays in the success or failure of any design project. In this chapter, I'll demystify the role of the designer in the branding process and walk you through the steps required to find a designer whose sensibility and methodology are likely to be a good fit for your organization.

The majority of good independent graphic designers work on a fairly broad range of projects; they tend, in that sense, to be generalists with agile minds and abundant creativity. If asked to work on the same old stuff day after day, they grow bored and frustrated. Why should that matter to you? Because the good news is that good graphic designers thrive on the kind of interesting communication challenges and diverse messages that typify the nonprofit sector.

You noticed I qualified my statements, right? I said *good* designers, because unlike plumbers, lawyers, or even the person who cuts your hair, graphic designers don't need to be certified in order to hang out a shingle. Consequently, there are vast numbers of quasi-professional designers out there.

Complicating matters, designers, like the rest of us, tend to have strengths and weaknesses: A great Web site designer may be a lousy brand designer, and the award-winning designer of annual reports may not have a clue how to design a decent ad. Then there are the designers who, although they say they do everything, may not do *anything* well.

Your challenge is to find a designer who is inspired, intelligent, and responsive to your needs. And to do that, you and your branding team have to know what you want and how to articulate it. (For help in doing just that, see chapters 2 and 3.) The following are some guidelines for finding the designer who is just right for you.

What to Look for When Reviewing the Designer's Portfolio

If the designer says, "We terminated the relationship with that client," or "The client wanted this. I thought it was the wrong approach. Yet, this was the design that was used," this could mean a lack of leadership or management skills on the designer's part.

There's no way around it: To find a design professional you feel comfortable with and whose work you like, you're going to have to interview a lot of designers and be able to evaluate the work they show you. But how do you, a non-designer, assess a design professional's portfolio? Here are some basic questions to keep in mind:

- Is the work in the portfolio consistently strong and organized in a way that's logical and speaks to your needs?

- Is there a design concept behind the work, or is the work merely decorative? You don't need decoration; you need design.

- Does the work need to be explained in order to be understood? The work should speak for itself.

- How much of the work was actually produced and how much is merely prototyped? Prototypes aren't proof that a designer can actually produce what he or she has designed. When work has been taken through the printing or manufacturing process and still looks great, you know you're talking to a pro.

- How much of the work relates to your organization's style? Is the portfolio just right—or is the balance off? Is it too serious or too whimsical, too modern or too classical? A good designer will hit the target for you stylistically.

The designer should show you examples of the kinds of materials—annual reports, Web pages, book jackets, logos—you're looking for help with. Not that you'll always know whether the examples are effective. Design is subjective, and what works and what doesn't is often a mystery even to an accomplished designer. What looks good to you may have been totally inappropriate and a flop for the actual client.

Here are some questions you might consider asking every designer you interview:

- How did your client define the design problem? Did the client provide a design brief? If not, how did you determine the objectives of the project?

- How do you present design concepts to your client? Do you show a tight, comprehensive presentation of one idea or loose sketches of several ideas?

- How did this particular design solution address your client's problem?

- How many applications did you create for the design program? May we see the whole program?

- Who acted as project manager—you or your client?

- Is the client currently using the design successfully?

The idea is to get insights into the designer's approach and working relationships with his or her clients. If the designer says, "We terminated the relationship with that client," or "The client wanted this. I didn't. I thought it was the wrong approach. Yet this was the design that was used," this could mean a lack of leadership or management skills on the designer's part. Besides helping you to determine whether the designer has talent, the portfolio review process is also an opportunity for you to learn about a designer's modus operandi.

Some designers insist on presenting only a single solution to a client—the right one. Others prefer to share their thinking in sketch form and proceed collaboratively from there, coming up with additional solutions based on a dialogue with the client. Either process may yield good results, but you need to figure out what you're comfortable with, and that includes deciding how much you need, and want, to be involved in the process.

But regardless of your level of participation, it's absolutely essential that you and your designer communicate; that's the key to establishing a good rapport. And that's the only way to succeed.

Selecting a Project Manager

Aaron Hurst, president of Taproot Foundation (*www.taprootfoundation.org*), organizes communications projects on a purely pro bono basis for select nonprofits in San Francisco and New York. "It's tough to judge designers by their portfolio. There are often several 'authors' in any project, making it hard to see what the designers are capable of by viewing their book," he notes. "So we often ask other professionals to recommend good graphic designers. It's not uncommon for us to find the project manager first, since they have links to the better graphic designers."

The best thing about working with nonprofits is that whether it's a museum, a school, or a performing arts organization, generally there is more "content" with which to get engaged. That makes all the difference.
— Michael Bierut, designer and partner at Pentagram

For all its projects, Taproot provides a pro bono manager who serves as the intermediary between the branding team and the client and is responsible for delivering the finished product on time, on budget, and on target. In other situations, the role of project manager may be filled by the designer or by a member of his or her staff, or by someone on the client's staff—a not-uncommon practice when the client is already providing other key players on the project who are not under the direct supervision of the designer.

So which is it? Will someone on your staff take on the role of project manager, or are you expecting the designer to fill that role? If you want the designer to be the project manager, be sure to evaluate your design candidates' managerial skills and acumen, not just their design talent. And don't forget to figure this added cost into his or her final design fee.

Other Considerations

Look for an indication of substantial design education on the designer's résumé. But be aware that it's only one factor, and education provides no guarantee that the designer has good design instincts. I've worked with amazingly talented designers who had virtually no formal design training. And I've met plenty of lousy designers with impressive degrees. The point is, really good design is often inspired, not learned. That said, designers are less likely to work in an idiosyncratic or spontaneous way and are more likely to follow a formal process if they have a design school background. So bring it up.

The size of a design firm is another consideration. Big graphic design firms or advertising agencies with in-house designers often have more resources to allocate to pro bono or low-fee nonprofit work than independent designers. In many ways, however, you get what you pay for, so be sure to find out from any designer under consideration exactly who will be working on the project and in what capacity. The last thing you want is to have your project delegated to a junior designer whose work falls short of your expectations.

Image 30. *This brochure was created in 1984, during the early years of the Brooklyn Academy of Music's Next Wave festival, at a time when various cutting-edge design agencies with distinctly different points of view would be commissioned to take on the institution's marketing materials.* Design: Doublespace. © 1984 Brooklyn Academy of Music

The Exception That Proves the Rule

The Brooklyn Academy of Music (BAM) is an important center of international avant-garde and classic theater, dance, and music. But in the 1980s, it had become best known for its very edgy Next Wave festival. This was a problem because "avant-garde" and "classical" are diametrically opposed concepts and the Philharmonic was becoming eclipsed. And what complicated BAM's identity further was the myriad of design approaches that the promotion took for BAM— none of which helped build a cohesive identity.

Image 31.
The Brooklyn Academy of Music (BAM) logo. Design: Pentagram. © 1995 Brooklyn Academy of Music

Pentagram was hired to design the BAM 1995 Next Wave brochure. Designer Michael Bierut's solution, much to the delight of BAM, made a big impression in a small cover space by lopping off the type. The chopped type also suggested "emerging talent." Bold stripes became practical devices to divide information in various marketing applications. This concept, the main element of which is the typeface, grew on BAM's creative management as appealing to both modern and classic audiences and has since evolved to become an integral part of the institution's brand identity.

BAM's identity (which is not logo-centric and, in fact, rarely uses its logo) is that the type—which is always News Gothic—is bigger than the space in which it exists, so that some of the letters are always "offstage." This is risky business because it means the creative director is challenged to constantly create something distinctive each and every time a new application of the identity is developed. Plus News Gothic is a $99 typeface that anyone may purchase so the design has to be unique enough to say "This is BAM." Sometimes the designer fails, sometimes the results are absolutely brilliant. But then, that's show biz.

There are exceptions to the rule (i.e., of cutting off the type), including the twirling BAM kiosk near the BAM Opera House. But BAM is about breaking rules and taking risks. And it really is wonderful to have an illuminated twirling kiosk on Flatbush Avenue in Downtown Brooklyn.

Interestingly, some firms seem to do their best work for nonprofits. With offices in London, Berlin, Austin, San Francisco, and New York, Pentagram (*www.pentagram.com*) is arguably the largest and most prestigious of the multinational graphic design firms. The New York office has created memorable brand identities for a number of local nonprofit organizations, including BAM (*www.bam.org*) and the Public Theatre (*www.publictheatre.org*). Michael Bierut, a partner in New York, says that almost two-thirds of his clients are nonprofits, representing mainly cultural and educational concerns, some large and well funded, like New York University (*www.nyu.edu*), and others small with modest budgets, like the Museum of Sex. Regardless of size or status,

Image 32. Branded BAMcafé paper cup. Design: Jason Ring, BAM (in-house). © Joanne Savio

Image 33. The twirling BAM kiosk on Flatbush Avenue, Brooklyn. Marquee design: Pentagram. Animation: Clara Cornelius, BAM (in-house). Photo: James Shanks. © 2001 Brooklyn Academy of Music

however, each client gets the same treatment. Says Bierut, "The best thing about working with nonprofits is that whether it's a museum, a school, or a performing arts organization, generally there is more 'content' with which to get engaged. That makes all the difference."

Steve Liska, president of Liska + Associates, whose current clients include Make a Better Place (see chapter 1), Hubbard Street Dance (*www.hubbardstreetdance.org*), the Racine Art Museum (*www.ramart.org*), and the Brain Research Foundation (*www.brainresearchfdn.org*), is also attracted to nonprofit work. According to Liska, about 15 percent to 20 percent of his work is for nonprofits, and a small amount of that is done pro bono. "We don't view nonprofits as charity, but we do view them as usually needing branding and communication design help more than anyone," he says. "They don't have the kind of media exposure that for-profits often do—so they need to be smarter and more focused. I think they chose us because we want to solve their problem to the best of our ability. Building a brand is always collaborative, and the process is no different for a nonprofit than it is for a for-profit client."

The Liska + Associates portfolio includes all the branding for Hubbard Street, a Chicago-based dance company. This is a re-branding for Hubbard. Liska + Associates first branded it more than twenty years ago. Besides clean and powerful graphics, Liska applies lots of exceptional photography to its design work, and Hubbard Street's branding is a prime example of that.

Image 34.
This large sign thanking donors hangs alongside smaller glass plaques that identify individual donors and patrons. Creative Direction and Design: Michael Bierut, Pentagram. Photo: Jason Ring. © Brooklyn Academy of Music

Image 35. *The BAM 1995 Next Wave brochure, designed by Pentagram.* Design: Michael Bierut, Pentagram. Photo: Timothy Greenfield-Sanders. © 1995 Brooklyn Academy of Music

What to Look for in a Proposal

In addition to a designer's portfolio and personality, before you make up your mind, you'll need to read the designer's proposal. So once you've narrowed the field of candidates to three or five, you should provide each with a design brief (see chapter 2). They, in turn, provide you with a written proposal based on the brief, usually within ten days. The proposal is important—for you and for the designer you ultimately hire.

Although design proposals run the gamut, from undesigned two-page estimates submitted via e-mail to multi-sectioned extravaganzas sent via FedEx, a good proposal should contain a description of the design process. Most designers follow a four- or five-phase process:

Image 36. BAM 20th Next Wave Festival Postcard. Design: Eric J. Olson, BAM (in-house). Photo: Jose Luiz Pederneiras. © 2001 Brooklyn Academy of Music

▶ Phase 1: Orientation (any background information or research is obtained)

▶ Phase 2: Design exploration (preliminary design solutions that address the project's objectives are developed)

▶ Phase 3: Refinement (when adjustments are made to the design as required by the client)

▶ Phase 4: Prepress production (the project is made ready for the printer/Web site host/ signage manufacturer, etc.)

▶ Phase 5: Printing or manufacturing (the project is taken to completion)

Look at these key components before making up your mind about which designer to retain:

▶ Points during the process when you will be allowed to approve/amend/reject the work in progress

▶ Time frames for each phase of the project

▶ What you, as the client, are expected to provide (i.e., copy, visuals, etc)

▶ Cost (i.e., the designer's fee plus an estimate of expenses)

Image 37. The large-scale application of the lobby kiosk for the Spring 2002 season directed at walk-in traffic and patrons. Kiosk Design: Pentagram. Creative Direction and Design (posters): Eric J. Olson, Clara Cornelius, BAM (in-house). Photo: Courtesy of Brooklyn Academy of Music. © 2002 Brooklyn Academy of Music

- Terms and conditions

- Biographies of the key players on the designer's team

- References (usually provided only upon request)

- List of relevant clients

- Portfolio of relevant work

A well-crafted proposal serves many functions: It reveals how the designers present themselves on paper; it provides a snapshot, for comparison, of how each of the designers sees the project progressing, as well as the roles they see you and themselves playing in the process; and it anticipates outcomes for each phase of the project. It also makes it easier for you and the designer to discuss problems up front, where they can be negotiated without bloodshed and/or needless expense. Best of all, it enables you to compare all of the designers as "apples to apples"—or "Macintosh to Macintosh," as the case may be.

Image 38. Harvey Lichtenstein was the man who transformed BAM into what it is today. At BAM, he is referred to simply and affectionately as "Harvey," and so that's how the theater got its name. Design: Pentagram. Photo: Elena Olivo. © 2000 Brooklyn Academy of Music

For all these reasons, I would be wary of short or incomplete proposals, since it may mean the designer has not thought through the way he or she wants to work with you. I would also be concerned about proposals that are not well designed. Think of the proposal as an extension of the designer's portfolio. If it's sloppy, thrown together, or unimaginative, you should ask yourself why you would want to work with a designer who isn't even tending to his or her own brand!

The design process is anything but routine. It's both unpredictable and exciting. In that sense, designers are constantly challenged to create something new.

Image 39. *Paula Scher, one of the Pentagram partners, designed the branding and many of the promotional posters for the Public Theatre in New York, including this one for* Bring in 'Da Noise, Bring in 'Da Funk. *Scher is a master typographer, and her style is extremely distinctive. But because branding systems require a lot of flexibility in order to remain effective over time, relying on the unique talents of one person can be a risky proposition. It's hard to imagine the Public Theatre asking some other designer to create in the same way as Scher—basically, to "do" Scher. Mimicry, while clearly the sincerest form of flattery, would be nothing to aspire to, from the perspectives of both the theater and the designer. So once Scher is no longer around, Public Theatre will have a challenge—to find a new designer to carry on who is different but as powerful and distinctive as Scher in style and approach.*

Terms and Issues

There are a fair number of boilerplate terms in the typical design proposal, and only a few—the deal breakers—usually get the client's attention and require negotiation:

- **Markups:** A carrying charge, usually 17.65 to 25 percent, for expenses incurred by the designer on the client's behalf.

- **Kill fee:** The fee, agreed upon in advance, received by the designer should the project be terminated at any point. The way the kill fee is calculated should be spelled out in the terms. Generally, the designer should be compensated for work done prior to termination.

- **Rights transfer:** While the designer generally transfers the copyright to the client for the completed brand identity when payment is made in full, he or she usually retains the rights to unfinished work or work not used.

- **Credit:** When appropriate, the designer generally wishes to be acknowledged in print for the work he or she has done. Such credit usually appears as a very

HUBBARD STREET DANCE CHICAGO

small, inconspicuous line of type somewhere on the piece and, when the work is exhibited (in design contests, for instance), also in the exhibition program.

In addition to copyright, the main legal and ethical issues of concern to designers are:

▶ **Work on speculation:** A designer should not be asked to create work without an agreement, on paper, that he or she will be paid and/or that the client, barring unforeseen circumstances, is intending to take the work to completion. This is a particularly thorny topic when it comes to pro bono work. If the designer is not being paid market rates, then the designer's only tangible compensation is to see his or her work realized, uncompromised.

▶ **Plagiarism:** A designer should never be asked to adapt and/or modify the work of another designer without that designer's knowledge.

▶ **Work for hire:** The independent contractor/designer should not be asked to give up his or her rights of authorship. Work for hire is a loophole (usually applicable to employees) in the copyright law, which, if agreed to in a contract, makes the creator all but invisible. An "all rights transfer," on the other hand, does not negate the creator's existence.

The Pricing and Ethical Guidelines (PEGs) published by the Graphic Artists Guild (*www.gag.org*) is the main industry tool for understanding per-project pricing, legal and ethical issues, and contractual terms and agreements; you should probably have a copy on hand if you'll be working with designers on a regular basis.

At the end of the day, most designers and clients are looking to create a simpatico relationship with their clients, one that rewards creativity and honest effort with appropriate compensation. The PEGs help clarify some of the issues relevant to that end.

Each side has to get what it needs for the relationship to thrive. Compensation, however, may not just be monetary and may also be defined by the designer to include:

- Satisfaction in seeing a project through to its successful conclusion

- Creative freedom

- Respect

- The knowledge that your work makes a difference

Simply by having read this book, you are helping to ensure that no matter how much (or little) you ultimately pay your designer, he or she is likely to be rewarded with other, less tangible (and often, more meaningful) forms of compensation.

Image 42.
Poster for Hubbard Dance. Design: Carole Masse, Liska + Associates, Chicago, completed in 2005. Art Direction: Kim Fry

Six

The Design Process: Taking It in Phases

> *The branding work we did made an enormous difference in our emerging public image.*
> *– Elyse Barbell Rudolph, executive director of the Literary Assistance Center, New York*

In chapter 4, I suggested that it's essential to honor the evolution of the design process. Skip a sequence and the process can fall off a cliff. That's why it's important, before you get started, to make sure the members of your design team are familiar with the various stages of, and roles they'll be expected to play in, the process.

Phase One: Research and Orientation

The initial phase begins after you have determined the members of the team and settled on a graphic designer. "But wait," I can hear you saying with some exasperation, "We already conducted our research. And isn't our design brief orientation enough?" The reality is, the designers will need to orient themselves regardless, but the fact that you've prepared a detailed brief should speed things along and save you money.

But while the brief may have served you well to this point, its existence is no guarantee that the design team you've chosen is ready to be fully engaged in the process. In fact, this is the moment when the team—and especially the designer—becomes immersed in the culture and values of your organization. For instance, it's a good time for the designer to rummage through your archives, where he or she may come upon that long-lost color palette or typeface that truly captures the essence of your organization. It's also a good time to go over with the designers the documents audit, including organizational materials (brochures, annual reports, letterhead) you've produced in recent years, noting the relative importance of each piece, any common language and brand elements they share, and whether individual pieces were considered successes or failures.

The Great Leap Forward

Image 43.
The former Literacy Assistance Center logo

The Literacy Assistance Center (LAC) logo had several fatal flaws—not the least of which was that it wasn't memorable. In fact, even those close to the organization couldn't remember what it looked like when I interviewed them. The typography was weak, and because the use of the logo was predicated on the size of the LAC initialism, it had to be huge in order to be legible, which meant the name, when it was spelled out underneath, had to be tiny. Even though the organization had only recently adopted the logo, when faced with the results of a brand survey, Elyse Barbell Rudolph, executive director of the Literacy Assistance Center, agreed with me that change was necessary. She says, "The branding work we did made an enormous difference in our emerging public image. As the center that supports one of the country's largest and strongest adult literacy networks, we have always enjoyed an excellent reputation in a rather small circle of colleague literacy organizations. Branding enabled a great leap forward in the quality of our public communications in print and online, so that we now find ourselves capturing the attention of people outside our field, particularly the media and government agencies and foundations generally not associated with literacy development. In the past few months, for instance, I have had several calls from reporters who were working on stories about the impact of immigration in New York, and this is partly a result of our work with the New York Times Company Foundation and the Mayor's Office of Immigrant Affairs—all due at least in part to the strength of our image having gone beyond our narrow field and out to a broader audience."

This is also the time for your designer to become familiar with other organizations in your corner of the nonprofit universe—competitors as well as those that can provide useful models in terms of successful branding systems. You can bet that when United Parcel Service re-branded itself recently, it paid close attention to the successful re-branding effort that Federal Express initiated a few years ago. While both UPS and FedEx changed their logos to be simpler and easier to read, they also realized that color was a key element of their branding systems and retained their brand equity: purple and orange in the case of FedEx, brown and golden yellow in the case of UPS, the color schemes that people had come to associate with each company. When you re-brand, you'll want to consider retaining any equity in your brand identity (if there is any) while differentiating it from your competitors. In order to pull that off, you'll need to develop an awareness of your organization's brand landscape.

After your designer and branding team have completed their research, the next step is to get the members of the team oriented. Orientation means identifying your organization's position vis-à-vis its competitors, partners, and the larger world:

▶ Are you a leader or an up-and-comer in your field?

Image 44.
Working with the design firm Whitehouse & Company, we surveyed the visual universe that LAC was a part of. As with most of the nonprofit sector, research revealed that that world was filled with weak brands. The good news: This made the job at hand a lot easier.

▸ What makes your organization and its offerings unique or vital?

▸ What makes your organization and its work relevant to its main constituency?

▸ Is its mission as relevant today as it was when the organization was founded?

▸ Where do you expect the organization to be in five years? In ten?

Your entire team needs to know the answers to these questions before you can proceed confidently to the design phase. Revisit your design brief in light of this additional work and, if necessary, challenge and/or modify the brief to ensure that it reflects the most current, accurate, and inspired picture of your organization (see chapter 2).

The Elevator Pitch

As you review the brief one final time with your branding team and your designer, develop a succinct positioning statement that sums up what your organization is all about. All the better if it can be said in one or two memorable lines—not only will it help you down the road with the development of a tagline, but it may also become the "elevator pitch" that you and your board members can use at appropriate moments, whether it's a cocktail party chock-full of potential donors or a chance encounter with an individual who would be a great addition to your board (see chapter 10 for more on the elevator pitch).

This is also the right time—and probably the last good opportunity—for everyone on the design team to speak his or her mind; introducing new information to the process after this stage often creates problems. New information can be almost anything, from "I forgot to mention that we're opening an office in India next year and the tagline has to work in Hindi," to "I neglected to mention that we can't use a cross or flame as part of our identity." Believe me, I've heard both.

Flushing out this kind of critical information at this juncture can save you time and money in the long run, while failure to do so inevitably will result in a demoralized and frustrated branding team. Remember, silence equals approval—so if you don't speak your mind, consider yourself guilty of "underminding" the process.

Identifying Brand Equity

Assuming it's not a startup, your organization probably has built up brand equity that it will want to preserve. Equity, in this context, means the elements of your branding that audiences readily identify with. The brand team at FedEx knew that people recognized and identified with the purple and orange in the company logo, but felt no such affinity for the name "Federal Express" because, among other things, it contained the word "federal," which had ambiguous connotations.

How will you and your team know when it's time to move on to the next phase of the process? First and probably most importantly, the designers will indicate that they have the tools and information they need to get started. But before you move on, be sure to summarize, on paper, all the observations and decisions the team has agreed on. Once that has been done, you can move on to phase two.

Phase Two: Design Development

Each designer has his or her own way of proceeding in this phase. In general, the designer will take all the information and decisions arrived at in phase one and, after a week or two, will return with sketches of several ideas for marks or "logos." Although "logo" (short for "logotype") once meant a text-only mark with a specific, customized typeface, it has now taken on a secondary definition, meaning simply an "identifying symbol," and is used interchangeably with "mark." The mark is positioned on a design continuum—from simple to complex, obvious to obscure, figurative to abstract. To avoid focusing on the logo in isolation, which can lead to more demands being placed on it than it can carry, these ideas are often shown in the larger branded context—for instance, logos applied to a Web site home page, T-shirt, and/or letterhead. Adding elements such as copy, illustration, and color makes it easier for you to understand how the logo interacts with these components, and the possibilities of the larger brand identity start to emerge. This will help you avoid taking the wrong direction.

Expressions of the brand should be presented as just that—ideas to be discussed, developed, or discarded. This way, each team member can feel comfortable revealing his or her views before a commitment is made to the overall concept.

The Literacy Assistance Center (LAC) is the organization that teaches teachers how to teach literacy in New York. Once the initial research was completed, I recommended several design firms to LAC; we chose to work with Whitehouse & Company. Together we surveyed the visual universe that LAC was a part of. As with most of the non-profit sector, research revealed that that world was filled with weak brands. The good news: This made the job at hand a lot easier.

Black-and-white sketches were presented to LAC and me by Whitehouse & Company with the pre-amble that "no idea is too dumb to be presented"— an approach that encourages open discussion from the entire team. Using the agreed-upon key words and phrases from the research phase ("dynamic," "professional," "innovative," "providing leadership"), we eventually chose several ideas for further development. My role at this stage is to help guide the discussion.

Image 45.
Black-and-white sketches for the new LAC brand

The second Whitehouse presentation, which I had art directed, included three of the ideas initially presented as sketches. Whitehouse & Company then developed them with me, and we showed them in color and in context—on the organization's letterhead—to LAC.

Image 46. *The second presentation of logos by Whitehouse & Company was narrowed down to three logos*

A totally different idea emerged from the second presentation to LAC, during which LAC talked about the primary importance of LAC as a resource hub and the ripple effect created in the larger community. The new idea, which was something of a departure for the team and the field, was embraced unanimously.

Next, a broad color palette was developed and each of the applications was designed and shown in a different color—blue for the letterhead, rust-orange for the business

Image 48.
The new LAC logo

card, brown for the mailing label, and blue-green for the envelope. The idea was to highlight the diversity of the population of New York City.

Whitehouse & Company applied the new LAC logo to a small black-and-white ad as well as

Image 49. The new LAC stationery system

to a mockup of LAC's Web home page. The photo on the site is of a young immigrant who spoke little English until she met and worked with one of the teachers trained by LAC. It was one of six photographs by Marian Goldman for LAC's annual report, which highlighted the idea that LAC is a community resource and is engaged in the important work of helping people with low or inadequate literacy skills to become more productive citizens. (The young woman in the photo is now in the process of getting a college degree.)

Image 50. The new LAC brand identity works well when applied to a small black-and-white print ad as well as the Web home page

Throughout the brand development process, I encouraged LAC's design team to model visual literacy by adopting a simple, uncluttered style—particularly on their Web site (www.lacnyc.org)—and clean, straightforward graphics in all of their branded materials.

The success of any branding program depends on buy-in—on how well everyone understands the brand strategy and whether they are willing to "get with the program." It's even more important in the typically nonhierarchical nonprofit setting to make sure that everyone is brought along as the design process unfolds.

So while it's to be expected that different designers will have their own style of presenting the work, I recommend including an educational component in the design process in order to nurture the feeling of inclusiveness. For instance, when working with a client, nonprofit or otherwise, Roger Whitehouse starts by discussing the brand identities of well-known heavyweights like IBM, Citicorp, the American Red Cross, or CBS. Each logo is explored in depth by both the branding team and the designer during the presentation. Before you know it, people start to relax (and defensive attitudes start to dissipate) as they begin to realize they share many of the same attitudes and opinions.

Image 47.
The staff of Whitehouse & Company. Left to right: Ben Whitehouse, Helga Whitehouse, Roger Whitehouse, and Saki Tanaka

This kind of session is often followed by a brief refresher—a review of the design brief that focuses on the particular components that define the nonprofit's identity, including the tagline, positioning statement, keywords, and elevator pitch.

Next, design ideas are presented as broad-stroke concepts—as points of departure that allow team members to jump in and have their say. Some designers may be horrified at this approach, especially if it's made to sound as if control of the process is being taken away from them. But what's brilliant about this tactic is that, if the designer's work is good (i.e., he or she has presented a range of solid ideas effectively) and the design team is working in earnest, it helps to further build the team spirit and promote buy-in. Unhelpful, emotion-based comments such as "I don't like red" or "I'm not comfortable with that typeface" are replaced by valuable insights such as "Red doesn't support the concept because it's too cautionary for our message of conflict resolution" or "This typeface is too modern for us; our organization needs to look more traditional because that reflects our mission statement."

Here are some key questions to consider while you're engaged in the design presentation phase:

▸ How valid is the concept for our organization?

▸ How powerful is the concept? Will our primary audiences connect to it on an emotional level?

▸ How original is the concept? Can we "own" this concept or is it too generic?

▸ Is the concept clear and focused or is it ambiguous? Can it be interpreted in more ways than one? If so, does it support our cause or undermine it?

▸ Is the concept versatile or rigid? Does it have "legs"— in other words, is it flexible enough to be used in a variety of ways that build a brand with depth?

▸ Can the logo be reduced or enlarged and still maintain its integrity? Can it be used in black and white and remain legible?

If I've given the impression that the process is in any way predictable, I've misled you. There are no formulas for arriving at a new brand identity—partly because most truly great identities break the mold or are somewhat unconventional.

By the end of the presentation, it should be clear which ideas work and which don't, and that's helpful for the designer as well as the team. What's more, remain open because sometimes totally new ideas will emerge from the discussion. As long as there is no expectation that a logo will be selected during the first meeting, the designer should be able to go away and come back, refinements or new ideas in hand, to a very positive, engaged, and informed committee.

Usually at this second presentation, team members begin to realize that their input has made a difference and, once the brand leader has given the nod to an identity, they can feel satisfied that the process has been inclusive and unified. Then, with any luck, there is the magical moment where it all clicks and the new identity is embraced. Says Roger Whitehouse, "The client representatives see themselves as important members of the design team and have entered into the process as genuine collaborators. In a sense, we never have a situation where the client chooses anything; instead, we all arrive at the same conclusions together."

If I've given the impression that the process is in any way predictable, I've misled you. There are no formulas for arriving at a new brand identity— partly because most truly great identities break the mold or are somewhat unconventional. But if it ain't predictable, or even particularly easy, it is the most exciting kind of journey to be on—especially if you are prepared to venture off the road from time to time in hopes of ending up at an even better place than you could have imagined before you set out.

How many e-mails do you get a day that fail to include a thoughtful and informative signature? How often do you get different e-mail signoffs from the same organization?

Let's face it, nonprofit e-mails are often too casual and unprofessional. A well-crafted signature, in contrast, shows the recipient of your message that you are accessible and organized. So consider the following components when creating the signature that's appended to the end of e-mails from you, the staff, or the board:

Name:

Title:

Organization name:

Tagline (optional):

Mailing address:

Phone number:

Fax number:

E-mail address:

Web site URL:

Upcoming events or any other relevant notice:

Typeface, spacing, and color are other important consider-ations and should be consistently applied throughout the organization. I use Arial because it's simple, clean, and a resident font on most computers, which means I can be pretty sure it will translate well in the e-mails I send out.

Seven

Finding the Sweet Spot: Arriving at a New Brand Identity That Everyone Can Embrace

In the previous chapter, I talked about how the initial design presentation may be used as a springboard for dialogue: A range of rough solutions may be shown to the design team as a way of stimulating discussion among team members. This can result in one or two ideas that the team wants to see developed further. But in some situations, a completely new idea may emerge that is even better than the designer's initial treatments. The important thing to remember is that you shouldn't expect the initial presentation to result in the perfect brand identity for your organization. And, in the worst-case scenario, it's back to the drawing board!

But how do you know when you've hit the "sweet spot" and found that unique visual expression of your brand-to-be, the one that will resonate with the greatest number of people? Because decisions in the nonprofit workplace are usually made by consensus, in some ways the task for a nonprofit is simplified: What any one member of the design team loves is irrelevant unless everybody else is able to "get on board" with it. Buy-in is essential to successful branding.

When it works as it's supposed to, consensual decision-making can lead to a stronger brand identity. Because the team, formed of individuals with different perspectives, represents the range of audiences you need to communicate with, when you do come up with an idea that speaks to most, if not all, members of the team, you can be reasonably sure you've found something that will appeal to a broad range of people.

Whatever you do, resist the temptation to share the design presentation with people in the office who aren't members of the design team. Doing so often signals a process that has gone off track and is at risk of failure, and it rarely results in useful feedback for the designer. Here's a rule of thumb I share with all my clients: The designer should be included when any aspect of the design presentation is being discussed. That's partly because while everyone is asked to look at the same thing, each person invariably sees it differently, and in many cases the designer is the only one who, for purposes of branding, sees it accurately. It's also partly to keep the project on a sound footing; opinions coming from left field can muddy the process.

Seeing with Our Brains

"Visual" thinkers (a category into which many people fit, including, of course, most designers) often make the mistake of thinking that others can see what they see. But because we "see" with our brains, not our eyes, the meaning of any image or design is subject to a spectrum of interpretations. While the visual thinker often sees things that are merely suggested (for example, a face or the shape of an animal in a cloud), the nonvisual thinker may tend to be more literal (i.e., a cloud is merely a collection of watery particles suspended in the atmosphere).

To better illustrate this phenomenon, take a look at some familiar logos:

- BP's "sunflower" logo is a very positive, organic symbol. The sun is a clean source of energy for almost every form of life. BP, which is actively engaged in developing alternative sources of energy, has changed its name in its advertising from "British Petroleum" to "Beyond Petroleum"—its tagline is "An Energy Company Going Beyond." Of the major energy companies in the United States (ExxonMobil, BP, Royal Dutch/Shell, and ChevronTexaco), whose logo stands out as forward-looking and distinctive? BP's. Consumers tend to gravitate to brands that promote a positive future, and BP's branding reflects a unique selling proposition that gives it a distinct advantage over its rivals.

Image 51. Do you know why British Petroleum (BP)'s new logo resembles a sunflower?

- The original Federal Express identity, developed by Fred Smith, the company's founder and chairman, needed to evolve. Because the company name was spelled out, the original Federal Express logo was long and placed on an angle (to suggest speed and liftoff). Its colors were blue-purple and red. The new brand identity developed by Landor Associates recognized the equity in the colors (adjusting and expanding the color palette) but found the angle as problematic. FedEx didn't want to lose the sense of movement, however, and so Landor made sure to include an arrow between the last two letters. Of the dozen executives in the room, Smith was the only one to see the arrow.

Image 52. Can you find the arrow in the FedEx logo?

- General Electric's logo first appeared sometime in the 1890s, when home appliances were GE's main focus. Later, "We Bring Good Things to Light" became the company's motto—an homage to the brilliant innovations of the company's founder, Thomas Edison. Today, GE's business reaches far beyond electric appliances; It's about aviation, automotive fleet lending, off-site storage, and broadcast media. In keeping with that diversification, the company's tagline has changed to "Imagination at Work," yet the GE logo remains static, promoting a somewhat antiquated look.

Image 53. Did you realize that the GE logo is the abstraction of an electric stove burner?

Recently I went through a presentation with one of my clients, Sisters of Charity of New York, a two-hundred-year-old congregation with an inspiring and courageous history. But the sisters who run the community are aging—as are many senior executives and leaders in the nonprofit sector today—and my research showed the congregation needed to reinvent itself in order to remain vibrant. There were approximately a dozen people in the first presentation, including the two design-firm principals who had been asked to design a new logo for the congregation, Craig Bernhardt and Janice Fudyma of Bernhardt Fudyma Design Group. By the end of the meeting, the sisters present at the meeting were happy about three of the treatments that had been presented—one featuring overtly religious imagery, the second an elegant but fairly radical abstraction, and the third somewhere in the middle—but were unable to choose one over the others.

Two weeks later, we re-presented to a larger group that included two sisters who had been unable to attend the previous meeting. Something was different this time: There was more enthusiasm for all three logo treatments than we had heard during the first presentation, even though most of those present were seeing

Image 54.
Craig Bernhardt and Janice Fudyma, principals of Bernhardt Fudyma Design Group

everything for the second time. Then one of the sisters who had not been at the first meeting began, in a soft voice, to explain what she saw in the most radical design: A hopeful future and God in the heavens. Amazingly, she also saw a cross where there was only the most vague suggestion of a cross (clearly, she was a visual thinker!), and the others saw it as soon as she pointed it out.

It was one of those moments when everything gels.

For Sisters of Charity, success in the future will depend on their ability to attract people from all cultures, faiths, and walks of life to their work—Muslims and Jews, as well as atheists. Given that reality, I suggested that it was perhaps better not to incorporate overt religious symbolism into their new brand identity. The sisters

in the room understood that, even if only intuitively, and they knew they were on the fence and needed someone from within the group, not a hired consultant, to help them get moving away from what they had always known and toward something new— and energizing.

Image 55. The new Sisters of Charity of New York business card

The atmosphere in the room was electric: People began to respond to the abstract design in a more confident way. Soon, new ways to apply it began to flow from those present and quickly a consensus emerged. Any anxiety members of the design team had felt previously

disappeared and they were unified in their decision.

Back in my office, some key lessons became clear. First, if you have someone in your organization who has visual acuity and is a team player, do whatever you can to get them involved in the design process.

Second, I was reminded that simplicity is almost always better than complexity. When I run across a complex, convoluted logo, I imagine someone on the logo committee saying to the designer, "Can you fit [pick a symbol] in there?" I call it the "kitchen sink"

Image 56. The new Sisters of Charity Web site features a photograph for each category; when you roll over the image with the cursor, it turns from sepia to full color to indicate which category you are entering. The tagline we developed is used here as a headline: "Living Lives of Love." It is an apt distillation of the charisma of their congregation: humility, simplicity, and charity.

approach to design, and it often comes from a place of insecurity. The logo doesn't have to do everything; it is the identifier and it has to do just a few things really well.

There is often a moment in the design process when someone with the respect of the team has to explain that a camel is a horse designed by committee. If the meaning of a symbol is not readily apparent, it may be best to stay with an abstraction or opt instead for an unembellished logotype (i.e., a modified type treatment of your organization's name).

Finally, never forget that, in the largest sense, branding is largely emotionally driven. Your objective is to hit the sweet spot—to find the combination of color, type, and design that feels right to you and your colleagues and that will resonate with your stakeholders and audiences, charging you up and helping you push to the next level.

Phase Three: Refining the Design

You've wrapped up phases one (research and orientation) and two (design development) of the design process, and now the designer is ready to go away and, based on your feedback, refine the selected logo.

This part of the process is like a funnel, a kind of narrowing down: You want your new identity to be as close to an exact representation of your organization as possible. Your job is to predict the uses of that identity (keep your documents audit close by) and to make sure your designer is very clear about what the identity needs to do. Any surprises should be pleasant ones.

When the designer is finally ready to return with the finished treatment, the presentation will be a bit different. The designer will probably want to show the logo in color and in various sizes, as well as applied to your letterhead and other applications including, perhaps, your Web site home page. Any changes at this point should be minor. With a little luck, your new brand identity will start to look real!

This is also the point in the process when you need to examine and revise language that is integral to the brand. In the excitement that comes with a new visual identity, it's sometimes easy to underestimate the degree to which language creates and reinforces audiences' perception of an organization. In fact, the copywriting function is usually an afterthought in nonprofit organizations. Don't make that mistake. Language, like design, is an important expression of the culture and character of your organization. If you can't afford to have a dedicated copywriter on staff, be sure that the people who create copy for you do so according to carefully thought-out guidelines—preferably guidelines that have been put in writing. For instance, do you present your organization as plainspoken or does it prefer a more authoritative tone? How do you want your audiences, internal as well as external, to refer to the organization? How are your values and your brand personality expressed in copy? How do you refer to the people who work for or with you (i.e., staff, volunteers)? These are all things you should discuss, design brief in hand, with members of the branding team. Remember, everything works to support or defeat the brand (see chapter 10).

The Importance of Visual Imagery

Although they try, most nonprofits fall short when it comes to using photography (and illustration) to expand and enrich their brands. Partly this is the result of poor planning: An event is scheduled, and everyone is so busy organizing it that, when the time comes, they forget to document it. Or the need may not be pending—until eight months later, when it's time to produce the annual report and staff is left scrambling for good images.

It's also partly due to a lack of imagination: Photos of "talking heads," tonsils on full display, can be deadly dull. On the other hand, if the photographer can capture a candid expression, create a special lighting effect, or imbue the image with a distinct point of view, that same moment may come alive.

The point is, don't leave the visual imagery associated with your brand to chance; it will only weaken the brand and hog-tie the designer. Instead, photography (and illustration) can and should be used, with all the collective forethought you can muster, to express the unique character of your organization and to differentiate it from its competitors and peers. Your designer can help with this. He or she should be able to establish broad guidelines for the use of imagery in your materials and be able to hook you up with photographers (and illustrators) capable of producing professional-quality work (see chapter 10 for more on this).

In talking with photographers, remember to be clear about your goals and requirements. A community development organization may want a photographer who excels at street scenes filled with movement, while a health care organization may need a photographer who takes powerful studio portraits. In either case, the photographer's portfolio should reflect his or her ability to produce the work required. I can't emphasize this enough: Lots of ideas that sound great can fall flat when realized, while some that sound outlandish or even foolish end up being just the ticket.

As you develop your organization's visual and written vocabulary, it will become clear that what you omit is as important as what you include.

Regardless of the choices you make, try to be consistent in the application of imagery to your branded materials. Remember, every decision you make has an impact on the overall effectiveness of your brand. As you start to develop your organization's visual and written vocabulary, it will become clear that what you don't do is as important as what you, in fact, do. This is when the brand starts to come alive. And once you perfect your stroke, you'll hit that sweet spot each and every time.

The Great ABC Logo Bake-Off

> Back in the 1980s, I was part of the small, young design firm of Ross Culbert Holland & Lavery. We found ourselves competing against goliath Landor Associates, the international brand design giant, to redesign the identity of the American Broadcasting Corporation (ABC). Landor had committed itself to one idea—an exclamation point.
>
> Our firms presented back-to-back to the logo committee, which was made up of a dozen high-level ABC executives. Roone Arledge, then president of ABC News, killed Landor's presentation with a few well-chosen words: "I can't use that on the air for the assassination of a president."
>
> Of course, they didn't choose either of our ideas either. Both picked up on the "American" in American Broadcast Corporation: One was an eagle ("NBC already has a bird") and the other a star ("Too generic. We can't own it."). Unable to decide how to proceed, the committee stayed with the original Paul Rand–designed logo, a circle with the lowercase "abc," which some ABC higher-ups had dubbed "the meatball." It is still the logo you see on air today.
>
> The point is, neither Landor nor our firm had been given the opportunity to bring the committee along in its thinking. The only time we met the key decision-makers

was the day of the big presentation, and I imagine that most of those on the committee had never thought about, much less been tasked with, choosing a corporate identity. To make matters worse, there was no time built into the process to allow the committee to thoroughly consider the ideas presented to it.

Ultimately, eighteen design firms were asked to help create a new identity for the network (plus design students from the Pratt Institute in Brooklyn, who were asked to submit logo ideas for free), yet it ended up with nothing, wasted massive amounts of money and time (six months), and demoralized a lot of people. All of which earned the project a dubious honorific in the design world—"The Great ABC Logo Bake-Off."

Eight

The Devil's in the Details: From Inspiration to Implementation

Once your new brand identity has been approved, you'll want to unveil it to your stakeholders (staff, board, and important volunteers). Take a moment to celebrate. But be aware that this is not a time to sit back and relax; the next stage of the process can be a minefield.

Your brand presentation should show your new identity in application—that is, applied to letterhead, brochures, Web pages, and so on—so that stakeholders don't focus too much on the logo, which is only one (albeit important) aspect of your brand. As you present the various elements of your new identity, be sure to repeat the keywords that informed the development of the brand; talk about the process. Reinforce the role the community played in developing the new look. Share any feedback that led you to a solution to a particular problem. Make it clear that the process was inclusive, not unilateral. It's important to get as many people as possible on board with the new identity. And nothing encourages buy-in like giving credit where credit is due: Target the people who can aid in the successful implementation of the brand (or bring it crashing to the floor) and speak to them one-on-one. Remember, each person has the potential to be your ally—or your nemesis.

Once the applause has died down, it's time to turn your attention to the mixed communications messages that have been holding your organization back. Before they go through the re-branding process, most nonprofits' collateral materials resemble a messy closet: brochures and letterhead are poorly designed and uneven in their production values and/or use of imagery and typography; Web sites tend to be a hodgepodge of content and sensibilities. Even if one or two of the pieces look good, the overall impression conveyed is one of confusion and disorganization. Absent a consistent voice, it's almost impossible to identify a unifying message.

There's a reason for this: Because nonprofits rarely have adequate resources to apply to their identity systems, identity tends to be an afterthought—and it usually shows. It's almost as if the saying, "you can have it good, cheap, or fast—you can get two out of three, which two do you want?" was coined for the nonprofit sector. Unfortunately, nonprofits that find themselves in a time or funding crunch usually opt for the cheap-and-fast approach to communications. But unless the brand identity is supposed to look down and dirty (in which case maybe it's a brilliant strategy), this kind of approach usually derails even the best-intentioned attempts to brand. Don't despair. I firmly believe that good design does not have to be expensive, and that the best brand identity is almost always a clear and simple one, regardless of the resources available. It all hinges on solid research and getting a good designer on board.

Many nonprofits, especially newer ones, rely on the kindness of strangers—or the connections of board members—when developing their logo and collateral materials. Branding is often not even an option. In these types of situations, it's not unusual for lots of people to get involved and for no one to truly take charge. Then, years later, after the organization has become a big success in spite of its chaotic, disjointed messaging, the board and/or executive director, having come to the realization that the organization can no longer go on this way, seeks professional help. Typically, someone suggests a documents audit. When the "closet" is opened, out topples a mess—a mess that you're expected to clean up. Then the idea of branding may enter the conversation.

It doesn't have to be this way. Organizations that start out the right way, with a good solid plan and the branding team to back it up, invariably save themselves time and money and are able to have greater impact, much faster. That most nonprofits don't seem to start out with a firm grasp of their brand identity and the discipline to execute it is a conundrum.

Don't make the same mistake. If you've been following my process, your organization is well on its way to developing an effective identity, one that your branding team and stakeholders are happy with and that you can start to apply to the materials on your documents audit list.

But How to Proceed?

How do you implement the brand? Keep two objectives in mind when thinking about how to proceed: 1) Be inspired—make each piece shine, create a documents system that has continuity, depth, and breadth; and 2) Be pragmatic—make sure to maximize the impact and utility of each and every piece created.

If you're the executive director and/or brand leader, you almost certainly will deal with staff and board members who are anxious to see where this process leads. Each one of them is likely to have a different mindset with respect to the organization and different attitudes about the process, and each one will bring some degree of creativity, skill, and ability to the table. In addition, many of them are likely to have been responsible for a communications piece that is going to be tossed. Don't be surprised if most gratefully accept the new brand, wanting the best for the organization, while a few do what they can (often unwittingly) to sabotage the process. If your nonprofit is relatively nonhierarchical in structure, as most are, then it's your job to make sure everybody's voice is heard.

Of course, experienced designers deal with this kind of tension all the time, understanding that, for many people, subjective opinions trump objective facts. And they know that since we "hear" with our brains, not with our ears, it's not unusual for people to take in information selectively and then interpret that information in a way that may not be useful. As Jane Zusi, associate creative director at Klemtner Advertising, a division of Saatchi & Saatchi Healthcare, says, "We've all had clients ruin our ideas at one time or another, Frankensteining things together."

Interventions

If a project shows symptoms of derailing, start with the following:

▸ Keep disgruntled staff and/or board members focused on the concrete goals and objectives of the new brand strategy.

▸ Remind them that the brand is not a personal statement.

▸ Keep repeating the keywords that were used to define the brand identity.

- Make sure the brand leader and brand steward roles are understood and observed by all.

- Accept feedback in a way that leaves the channels of communication open.

- Summarize feedback for the brand leader; the brand leader should be the ultimate decision maker, while listening carefully to the larger group.

You want to tap into, not discourage, the collective wisdom of the group. But even though yours may be a nonhierarchical organization, that doesn't mean it's a democracy. Each person needs to be reminded (gently) to focus on his or her specific role and give feedback appropriately. Anyone who doesn't have a role in the process should be encouraged to make his or her views known to the person in charge. That person, in turn, will decide what to do with the feedback. At no point, however, should feedback be given—or solicited—outside the structure created for that purpose. The more it is, the more likely the process will degenerate into mob rule.

A Case Study: Re-Branding Aish HaTorah

Recently, Aish HaTorah ("Fire of the Torah"), a large international membership organization that promotes the Jewish faith to young people, came to the realization that, in terms of its communications messages and vehicles, it had a very messy closet indeed. Over the years, each of the organization's eight branches had gotten into the habit of developing its own collateral materials, with some branches doing a better job than others. The result was a weak, almost nonexistent brand for the organization—and a lot of frustration for its executives.

At some point along the way, the organization's New York branch found an angel: Lynn Altman, brand expert and head of Viverito + Brandmaker Express.

Because she works primarily with large corporations, Altman, who describes herself as a "not-very-practicing Jew," decided to take on the job of re-branding the New York branch on a pro bono basis, figuring that if "I volunteer my personal time and skills by teaching karate to disabled adults, why not donate my professional time and skills by helping a nonprofit with its branding needs?"

Altman first identified college students, singles, and young married couples as Aish HaTorah's primary audiences. In doing so, she also realized that those groups were less receptive to an obviously "Jewish" brand than their parents or grandparents might have been. Her solution to the problem was to create a brand identity for the organization that eschewed obvious Jewish iconography (e.g., the Star of David or Hebrew letterforms). Instead, it relied on subtle "cues" and a series of humorous taglines (for instance, "All of the Fun; None of the Guilt") to signal Aish's upbeat, sophisticated attitude and strong connection to the Jewish faith.

The new branding system, which was designed by the Bernhardt Fudyma Design Group of New York, provided a variety of approaches (depending on the audience) that could be applied to business cards, letterhead, brochures, and all sorts of other materials. It also called for the organization to shorten its name to Aish, which had already been used informally by several of the organization's branches.

Realizing that brand and message continuity was important to maintain across the organization, Aish's leaders convened executives from its eight branches to compare their collateral materials. After some discussion, they decided that the system developed by Altman and the Bernhardt Fudyma Design Group for the New York branch was the most effective and agreed to adapt it across the organization.

The brand guidelines developed for Aish (see appendix A for the entire guidelines) describe and illustrate how the organization should apply its new identity to its collateral materials: what typeface families to use; the concept behind the color palette; how imagery should be used; how copy should be written to tie in to the concept; and so on. And while many different application examples are included, they all express the brand by sharing the same humorous sensibility and are presented in a way that illustrates the depth and breadth that can be achieved within a robust, consistently branded identity. Though you may not need to go to these lengths to create your brand guidelines, you should strive to accomplish the same thing.

A useful exercise: Think about how the brands you're familiar with have evolved over the years. Compare ads in old issues of your favorite magazines with the way those same products or concerns are presented today. What has changed? What has remained the same? More often than not, you'll notice that while the look of the most durable brands may evolve and change over time, the organization's core message almost always remains the same.

Image 57. Aish's
untidy closet. Below,
everything has been
redesigned and
rewritten to reflect
the new Aish brand

Image 58. Aish's
extreme makeover.
See appendix A for
the complete Aish
branding guide

Nine

The Big Switcheroo: Implementing Your New Brand

So, you have a new logo, letterhead, and related materials. Congratulations! You're ready to unveil your new brand to the world. Or are you? It's really a matter of logistics. And a big part of the decision rests on how the change will be perceived by your board members, supporters, and constituents. The piecemeal approach could look sloppy if the change is dramatic. But if the change is subtle, why not just wait till you need to replace letterhead? At any rate, you need a thoughtful plan. Here's a case in point.

Organizing for Change

Back in the early 1960s, the Swedish government released the results of a series of studies that demonstrated that driving on the right side of the road increases motorists' field of vision and, in effect, overall traffic safety. After extensive national debate on the issue, the Swedish government made the decision to switch the country's motorists from driving on the left side of the road to driving on the right. But it didn't implement the change until 1967, and when it did, it chose 6 A.M. (rush hour!) on a clear, crisp morning to make its big switch. Why did it take so long for the Swedes to implement the change? And why did they decide to implement it all at once—and during rush hour, no less?

For starters, the Swedish government had examined everything that might be affected by the change. And it realized, for one thing, that they needed new buses with doors that opened on the right. After further study, the government decided it would take a few years to get everything in place to make the transition. At the same time, the government also considered various strategies for introducing the change and finally decided that the surest way to get motorists' attention and safely reorient large numbers of people to what, was after all, a drastic shift in their driving habits, was to do it during rush hour. A perfectly reasonable assumption.

The results: there weren't many accidents as a result of the change, but a few people had a difficult time making the switch, particularly the elderly. Those who couldn't cope at all simply stopped driving.

Sweden's experience provides us with a rich metaphor for nonprofits that are at that stage of the re-branding process where they need to consider the timing of the switch to their new brand identity. In other words, when *should* you make the switch? After the printer delivers your new letterhead? Maybe. But what do you do with the old brochures that have yet to be replaced? Include a copy with every letter that goes out on the new letterhead? Or will that look unprofessional or confusing? What

Image 59.
One morning at rush hour, Swedish authorities decided to make everyone drive on the right-hand side of the road

about your Web site? Has it been redesigned to reflect your new brand identity? And just imagine the potential for confusion if your new identity involves a renaming of the organization as well as a fresh, new identity.

Recently, the New York City–based Alliance for Nonprofit Governance adopted a new brand identity of its own. This almost 100 percent volunteer organization works to raise the standards of governance among nonprofit organizations, particularly in New York, and has a diverse membership that ranges from consultants, academics, lawyers, and accountants to funders and a wide range of nonprofit practitioners. It is also an organization that takes its role as a model of good governance very seriously. As part of its re-branding effort, the marketing and branding committee (one I sit on) decided to recommend changing its name to Governance Matters.

Alliance for Nonprofit Governance

Image 60.
The original Alliance for Nonprofit Governance logo

The organization, which is only a few years old, decided to make the change after it realized that, thanks to the length of its name, it was forever doomed to be known as ANG—a meaningless initialism that some members pronounced as "A-N-G" and others shortened to "ang," as in "bang." In contrast, the phrase "governance matters" had been used in several of the organization's programs since its founding and, as organization vice chair Anne Green recalls, "perfectly captured the motivation of all those who labored in those early days to get ANG off the ground."

Of course, the new name had to be approved by the full board, which strongly backed an inclusive process as a way of securing buy-in from all board members. To accomplish that, the presentation of the new identity was preceded by a one-on-one discussion of the new name, giving board members a chance to air their concerns privately. As a result, the presentation to the full board was a virtual fait accompli, and any tension that might have been created by a sudden unveiling of the new name was replaced by almost universal enthusiasm for the change at the board level.

What to Do When Complications Arise

Not all of the ramifications of a new brand identity are directly related to design or marketing concerns.

Also, it's important early in the process to try to identify all possible snags to minimize the fuss and expense required to address them. For example, one ANG board member with a solid grasp of the organization's bylaws recognized that the organization's name change could only be ratified by a clear majority of its entire membership. Among other things, that meant the ANG board would have to wait for the organization's annual meeting to ratify the new name. But then ANG's pro bono attorneys pointed out that New York State does not require a majority of the entire membership to vote on corporate changes and recommended that the board amend the organization's bylaws, in accordance with state law, to allow two-thirds of the membership present to vote on corporate changes in the future. The board agreed, and the members also voted to change the bylaws accordingly at the annual meeting.

In preparation for the annual meeting, ANG sent a notice to its members explaining the rationale for the name change, including the fact that a trademark search had revealed that the name was available in the nonprofit category, should the organization choose to protect the name, and that both the domain names *governancematters.org* and *governancematters.net* had

GOVERNANCE MATTERS

GOVERNANCE **MATTERS**

Image 61. The new name is a play on words and provides many opportunities to express the two meanings, each of which works for different situations

Image 62. Notepads were handed out at the ANG annual meeting announcing the day of the name change

been secured. The mailing encouraged them to send their feedback. As with the board, it's important to give the members early notice of any actions and therefore give them a chance to absorb dramatic and/or important changes in an organization's identity.

The vote on the name change was taken at the annual meeting on February 1 (it passed unanimously), following a PowerPoint presentation of the new identity system. We announced that the marketing committee would be rolling out the new Governance Matters brand, "Swedish style," on May 1, after the Web site, letterhead, and collateral materials had been redesigned to reflect the organization's new identity (see appendix D). As a final touch, at the meeting's close, all members present were given Governance Matters

Image 63. Governance Matters' e-newsletter, designed by Bernhardt Fudyma, is used for announcements and news for the organization. Images were gathered from the member organizations (in this case, the Environmental Defense Fund).

notepads in a wrapper that said, "Do not use until May 1." This was followed by the celebratory cutting of a cake decorated with the new logo and the donning of T-shirts (of course, with the new logo) by all board members.

A New Vocabulary: Words and Visuals

The branding committee of ANG also took a long, hard look at the copy that was featured on the organization's Web site and in its key brochures. Prior to the formation of the committee, most of that copy had been written by various individuals or "by committee." In other words, the organization had no systematic way of approaching the written word. This, I'd hazard a guess, is fairly typical in the nonprofit

Image 64. The home page for the Governance Matters Web site also uses a rotation of images from member organizations as a way to express the effect of good governance

sector. But in creating a marketing and branding strategy for ANG, this too had to change, and we hired a professional copywriter to develop a tone and approach for the organization's key communications pieces—including frequently asked questions (FAQs), the body copy for its main brochure, and the main copy for the Web site.

ANG had used almost no visuals on its Web site, brochure, or other collateral materials. So the branding committee started to identify opportunities where visuals (charts, maps, graphs, photographs) would help clarify what the organization was all about. This is an area that the organization will continue to develop as it reinvents itself as Governance Matters.

Brand identities are living, breathing things, and as such, they require lots of love and attention.
— Bart Crosby, brand designer

The Gestation Period

Between the time ANG realized it would probably be making this monumental change and the approval of the new name by the membership (about eight months; the renaming process itself took about four months), the organization applied for and received five grants that were applied to the brand identity, redesign of its Web site, and other collateral materials. A year prior to that, a committee of six was formed to tackle the re-branding effort, so, altogether, the entire process took almost two years. That might sound like a long haul, especially considering that the effort was staffed almost exclusively by volunteers, but what kept the team from getting stalled, sidetracked, or otherwise turned around was a clear, engaging process and the gumption to stick with it.

Do you have the equivalent of Swedish buses to change before launching your new brand? Is there an aspect of your re-branding effort that will require extra time to change? What about other repercussions? Do you have board members who are wedded to the old brand and way of doing things? What about other stakeholders and audiences? Do you know how they will react to your new brand? If you haven't thought about it, now is the time to start.

As designer Bart Crosby says, "Brand identities are living, breathing things, and as such, they require lots of love and attention." Recently, a client of mine presented its new and stunningly handsome identity to its entire body of constituents, several hundred people. Each person was asked to write down his or her initial impressions. Even though the new identity was presented by the organization's president and generally well received, of the seventy people who chose to submit comments, roughly fifteen had something negative to say. It was a shock to see how differently these people viewed the identity. Most loved the color palette, but a few hated it; many responded to the abstract design as if it were a Rorschach and read all manner of things into it— most were positive, a few were negative. I imagine that, as with Rorschach tests, this reflected the observer's personal worldview.

That's the way a lot of brand presentations go, but in most situations, no one has the presence of mind to ask for candid, anonymous comments from those in attendance. The reality is that not everyone is going to understand the choices you made for your new brand identity, and not everyone is going to agree with your decisions. In fact, similar to what happened in

Sweden on that clear, crisp morning some forty years ago, some people will simply stop driving. That's okay. If you've done your homework and laid the groundwork, most people will embrace your new brand and happily make the switch—and will be better off for it.

Ten

Storytelling and the Brand: A Thousand Words . . . and Loads of Pictures

There are ways to improve your own writing skills that will make the task of creating copy easier, will make you a more critical reader, and, in the process, enrich your life as well.

Once an organization has established its new identity, the ongoing task of the branding team is to make sure that that the brand is nurtured—that it remains fresh, effective, and on message as the brand story evolves. And when you get right down to it, words and images are the two main tools at your disposal to tell your story.

Places where you will tell your story include:

► Advertising (print, radio, and broadcast)

► Annual reports

► Business cards

► Grant proposals

► Electronic or printed newsletters

► Event flyers and invitations

► Packaging

► Press releases and kits

- Posters

- Program brochures

- Public speaking engagements

- Signage

- Reports

- Thank-you notes

- Web sites

But DK, you ask, who's going to do all this writing and take all these pictures? Who is going to tell the story?

For small nonprofits, the easy answer is that it's a shared responsibility. And often there is no choice. But writing by committee, like design by committee, means no author crafts an inspiring vision—or takes blame when the vision goes awry.

And the biggest problem with this approach is that committee writing almost always ends up diluting or confusing the brand message. How many times have you puzzled over an organization's message after reading its brochure or flyer copy? Writing by committee, I guarantee it! The same is true of images. If the photos and visuals applied to a brand don't convey a distinct point of view, you can be certain that the brand will seem fuzzy, conflicted, or generic.

In situations where writing by committee is unavoidable, identify the writer(s) whose style best fits the tone that you want to achieve, and then support that person in developing the main copy. It's a good idea to keep your designer (whether pro bono or paid) involved in this process, as he or she will usually be the person with the most brand experience. Once the tone is established, other writers can step in and help out with the more ancillary needs of the brand.

Your designer can identify appropriate and innovative ways to express ideas by combining words and images, and can guide you in that process. That's what designers do. And often, the process of design starts with copy that expresses an idea that then becomes the springboard for an ad campaign or brochure or poster design.

Beyond that, there are ways to improve your own writing skills that will make the task of creating copy easier, will make you a more critical reader, and, in the process, enrich your life as well.

Copywriting 101

Since the ability to write well is a necessary skill in most nonprofit workplaces, it makes sense to ask potential members of your brand team to submit writing samples if they are likely to produce copy for any of the projects on the laundry list at the beginning of this chapter.

For those whose writing skills could use some polishing, here are a few tips that will get them up to speed.

Create an outline. Before you sit down to write, review your organization's mission and values statements and create a list of essential words, ideas, and phrases that you want to incorporate into your copy. Consult your design brief for ideas as well. Then make an outline that prioritizes the messages you'd like to convey. Only when you have those things in hand are you ready to begin writing.

Learn to tell a story. People have an easier time understanding stories, since they use concrete imagery and a story is usually about people; therefore, they can see themselves in the situation. Quite often copy is abstract and doesn't lead the reader to become engaged. A good story paints a picture that makes a clear and compelling point and thus leaves us with a lasting, motivational message.

Find a comfortable style. Often the way a person writes is far different from his or her speaking voice. Often people stiffen up or "bland out" when they write. That's unfortunate, because an authentic style can be easier to read and is often livelier. While making sure you are honoring the agreed-upon style, the keywords, and the values of your brand, develop a writing style that can be easily digested and appreciated by your audiences.

Pay attention to style and tone. The style and tone of anything you write should reflect the values inherent in your brand. If your organization is creative and nonhierarchical, the style and tone of your written materials should reflect that fact. Conversely, if your organization is more traditional and buttoned-down, you don't want to become too informal in tone in your copy. Your team needs to agree on the style you want to achieve before any writing starts.

Look it up. It's hard to use a word correctly if you aren't certain what it means. Get in the habit of looking up words when you're not clear on their definition. By becoming more confident in your use of words, you will be much more likely to develop a writing (and speaking) style that is natural, not forced.

Here are a few other tips:

- Be consistent in your use of tense

- Use the active (not passive) voice

- Be succinct; eliminate redundancies and irrelevancies

- Edit ruthlessly—cut, cut, cut!

- Most of all, remember what you stand for—the essence of your brand.

It doesn't hurt to keep a copy of William Strunk Jr. and E.B. White's *The Elements of Style,* currently in its fourth edition, within arm's reach. This short, wonderfully written style guide delves into the mysteries of composition and, through the use of dozens of examples, answers some of the nagging questions we all have about grammar and punctuation. Toward the back of the book, you'll find a list of twenty or so pointers on how to develop your own style—great advice even for seasoned writers!

When to Hire a Pro

So you've given copywriting the old college try, and the results are still less than scintillating. Don't be disheartened. There will be occasions, even for small nonprofits, when a professional writer is the best option. Recently, for example, I worked with a group of volunteers (i.e., as part of the branding team) that had been tasked with writing promotional copy for the nonprofit with which they were affiliated. But with the deadline looming and no one able to devote the time needed to come up with copy that was compelling, we decided the best option was to hire a professional. Once the writer established the tone and style, we would take it from there to develop the rest.

So, over the next week, we determined our budget for writing, interviewed four writers (each submitted writing samples and an estimated fee), and finally chose someone who was a global thinker and who could create copy fast and efficiently. Barbara Krasne, principal of KrasnePlows, executive management consultants, says, "So often, a hiring decision is based only on who you know or who is recommended, not the quality of the candidate's work. Make sure that you review writing samples carefully, focusing on the text itself. That way you can make sure that the copywriter fits your needs. Don't get distracted by the layout or design. It is not relevant. Then check references thoroughly to determine if that person's work is stylistically compatible with your own internal processes."

We provided the chosen writer with clear guidelines and selected examples of what we had done before. (Don't use the kitchen sink, "Let's give them everything we have ever done and let them wade through it" approach, since that invites speculation and interpretation.)

Also, we made one person the liaison with the writer. Everyone read the copy as it was submitted, then commented to the liaison, who distilled the comments, decided what the corrections should be, and communicated all that to the writer.

Nonprofits have a notoriously high rate of revision because so many people are involved in the process. This drives the cost of the writing up, makes for a chaotic process, and, ultimately, sours the relationship with the writer.

Stephanie Fritsch, president of Stephanie Fritsch Communications in Montclair, New Jersey, says, "Where experienced writers excel is in their ability to hone information and strike the right balance. Provide lots of detail without becoming dry. Speak to several audiences with one clear voice. Keep it fresh and lively without becoming promotional. Or express emotions without making it a painful read. A professional tends to work from the readers' perspective, and that can make a big difference in how engaging and effective your materials are."

Creating a Visual "Voice"

What many nonprofits don't realize is that visuals are just as important as words in expressing an organization's brand. I have worked with nonprofits that used no images—no photography, charts, illustrations, or maps—in their collateral materials, not a one! And after a few meetings with the executives of those organizations, the reason became painfully obvious— they were blind! They had no concept of the importance of imagery in their materials, and had no visual thinkers on staff. How could they tell their story in a compelling way without the support of visuals?

Every brand leader should be aware of the visual acuity of the members of the branding team. (See chapter 4 for more about branding teams.) Since non-visual thinkers may have a harder time understanding visual concepts, it may be difficult for them to appreciate the contribution a visual "voice" can make to furthering the organization's message.

An investment that helps solve this problem is a digital camera and staff members trained to use it properly. This is because, in order to tell your story, many events should be documented with an image. For example, a new staff member comes on board and you want to put his or her shining face on your Web site; or you just redesigned the office reception area and you want to show it off; or your new board chair addresses the membership and you need a picture to go with the excerpt of his or her speech in the newsletter. These are all expressions of your brand. And with your digital camera at the ready, you will have them to use when you need them.

Digital photography is increasingly more affordable and fast. It's also easier to use than conventional photography—both in printed materials and on the Web—simply because it is already digitalized; no scanning of images is required. It's also more reliable because you see instantly whether or not you have the shot you need. No waiting for film to develop. Other things you need to know about in order to take effective shots include cropping, composition, and lighting. While trial and error is often the best teacher, there is no shortage of downloadable step-by-step tutorials online (e.g., digital photography for dummies). So make the small investment, and then have the camera charged up and ready to use, and you'll get the shots you need.

In addition to these quick shots, you will want to consider other sources of imagery. Whether hiring a professional or buying stock, images can take the following forms:

▶ Photography

▶ Illustration

▶ Charts

▶ Maps

For many nonprofits, taking photographs is reserved for portraits of key staff, board members, and important events. In the case of the latter, these needn't be boring shots of talking heads or groups of attendees chatting over a chicken lunch. Instead, they should be treated as opportunities to truly express your brand. Be creative!

Image 65. The ASMP Web site

But if there is no one on staff able to take on this task, how do you find a good photographer? One way is through your local chapter of ASMP, the American Society of Media Photographers. The national ASMP Web site (*www.asmp.org*) also has a feature called "Find a Photographer" that enables visitors to the site to search for professional photographers by city, state, or country, as well as specialty. Or you may look through the source books like *Workbook* (*www.workbook.com*) or *Showcase* (*www.showcase.com*). Source books are the main ways to find photographers or illustrators at this point. They publish the work of creatives who have paid to have their work included in the publication (and/or on a Web site). All contact information is provided, and many photographers or illustrators pick up their own phones.

Workbook has been the largest of these books for some years

Image 66. *The Workbook Web site*

now and contains the widest range of style among top talent. On the downside, most sourcebooks do not jury the work between their covers (or on their affiliated Web sites), making it difficult for the novice or nonvisual thinker to discern good work from bad, derivative versus original.

For those who are likely to feel more comfortable with work that has been evaluated by others, *Communication Arts* magazine (*www.commarts.com*)

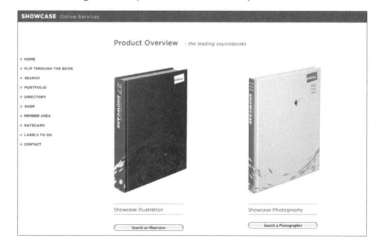

Image 67. *The Showcase Web site*

publishes illustration and photography annuals. All work included has been selected using the jury process.

Working with any creative person can be a unique experience, so it's hard to make generalities. That's why it's important to compare several portfolios before deciding on one. Pick a good photographer or illustrator who is both a good listener *and* sympathetic to your cause. You should tell the person what you are going for—both in concept and in practical application—but be aware that you are simply providing a guideline.

A good photographer (or any creator, for that matter) should improve on your idea by seeing opportunities where you cannot. Photographer Marian Goldman says, "My attitude is the same for all my work. Just because I may be shooting for a nonprofit and getting less money, that doesn't mean that I will hold back any of my skills or energy needed to do a good job. Occasionally, you need alternatives, though, if the concept costs too much extra money. For example, when DK Holland and I worked on the Literacy Assistance Center annual report, the original idea was to create portraits of each of the five people profiled in their homes to add a bit of their environment to the picture. This would have cost a lot of extra money in transportation alone, so we decided to do it all in my studio and add a little something from everyone's life to the shot, which worked out beautifully. We were able to get great expressions from all of the subjects, and everyone had a fun time being in the studio."

Pricing depends on how busy the photographer is, what equipment is required for the assignment, the time needed for scouting locations, assistants, and/or studio time. To better understand what you'd be getting for your money, you should ask for a rationalization of the fee that's quoted to you.

Fees are usually based on rights granted. Photographers (and illustrators) are keenly aware of the rights they are entitled to under the copyright law (typically much more so than designers or writers), and base their fees on granting rights—usually "one-time use" or "all rights." Obviously, if the photograph (or illustration) is of your board chair, the photographer or illustrator is not going to expect to be able to resell that image to anyone but you. If your agreement is for use in your annual report, don't automatically think you can also use them online without an agreement.

When your budget or time constraints won't allow you to hire a professional, stock photo agencies such as Corbis (*http://pro.corbis.com*) and Getty (*http://creative.gettyimages.com*) offer dozens of categories and tens of thousands of stock photographic or illustration images. FotoSearch.com takes advantage of the ability to search many sources to provide you with seemingly limitless options for imagery.

Although frequently overlooked, original illustration is often just the right solution for establishing a mood or conveying an abstract concept that can't be photographed easily (or inexpensively). And professional illustrators are also happy to create charts or maps—although more complex maps are likely to require the talents of a cartographer.

A picture may be worth a thousand words, but are they the *right* words?

You Have to Know Your Story to Tell It

The brand is never static. You have to recognize how your story is changing, to discuss the shift so that you can make a conscious and strategic change in the brand to accommodate. To do this intelligently, you need agreement on how the story is evolving. For instance, in chapter 1, I talked about MoMA's and

Make a Better Place's adjustments to changes. In both cases, the way they told their story changed as they evolved. Their ability to tell their changing stories well kept their audiences engaged, rather than confused and, therefore, disinterested.

But in order to do any of this, you need to know your story to begin with. The bare bones of the story may include how your organization started, who started it, who it serves, how it is proceeding to tackle its issues, and why it's important that it exists.

Reinventing the Elevator Pitch

The "elevator pitch," as traditionally understood, is a canned statement that describes your story—the "who, what, why, where, and how" of your organization—in the space of a short elevator ride. But the traditional elevator pitch is a less-than-useful concept for nonprofits. The implication is that someone of interest to you is unexpectedly stuck in an elevator with you—a short-term captive. But in reality, most people don't want to be pitched to (and, after all, nonprofits are not selling vacuum cleaners door to door), and no one is truly captive. Your story will only stick if a real connection has been made once the elevator door opens. But the real point of an elevator pitch is about maximizing time in unexpected situations and, because of that, you do need to synthesize your organization's message. Keeping all this in mind, turn "elevator pitch" into "elevator conversation," and you'll establish the connection with the other person because he or she is engaged (i.e., not being "pitched").

One way to do that is to create a short, provocative answer to the inevitable question, "What's your organization about?" You might respond by using just a half-dozen keywords or phrases that sum up your organization in a natural, inspiring, or provocative way. If the person's eyes light up, follow with something like, "Do you know _____?" [Fill in the blank with a short phrase that describes your primary audience or focus.] If the person answers, "Yes, I do!," this is a further opening to respond, to ask and take more questions, to have a discussion. Continue with the dialogue (and avoid switching to a monologue). But if the person doesn't respond at all, find another way to engage or consider that there may be no reason to continue the discussion anyhow. In which case, save your breath for another person. By the time the elevator opens, if you have been successful, you've gotten across the four or five key points about your organization in a memorable way and a relationship has been formed. Your story has been told. Cards have been exchanged. "May I call you?" has been asked and answered. That's what branding is—effective communication through a *common* language. And because you get instant response, telling your story verbally is a great test to see how others respond, so you can fine-tune before it works its way onto your Web site, or your annual report.

As the story evolves, the constants of the brand are the name, tagline, typography, logo, and color palette. The brand steward's ongoing role is to make sure the current strategy stays on track; the brand leader's role is to keep his or her finger on the pulse of the brand, to alert the brand team that the story is changing, even in subtle ways, and to act accordingly.

Do You Need to Trademark?

How do you decide whether you need to register your name, tagline, or program titles as trademarks? The trademark law enforced by the United States Patent and Trademark Office (www.uspto.gov) is designed to protect the consumer—and, in effect, the creator as well—against confusion in the marketplace. These protections are extended to nonprofit organizations involved in commerce (goods or services) of some kind (i.e., conferences, pro-grams, publications, products, and so on).

As soon as you provide goods or services (and not until then), you automatically have a common law trademark. You don't have to register at all. But you do need to consider registering your trademark if you are concerned about possible confusion. For instance, with trademark protection, you have the right to tell another entity (who's using the same name in the same marketplace) to stop using the name, thus eliminating the confusion.

When it comes to protection, it's often a matter of who got there first. And you can register a trademark for only a few hundred dollars. You can fill out the forms yourself but Lori Lesser, an intellectual property partner with Simpson Thacher & Bartlett LLP, says, "The law requires organizations to perform a 'clearance search' before using any new trademark, to ensure that the same trademark or a confusingly similar one is not already being used by someone else. To be safe, such a search should include prior registered and unregistered trademarks. It is prudent to involve a lawyer in the process for two reasons. First, a layperson is unlikely to know all the resources to consult for such a search. Second, while a layperson can spot a prior trademark that is an exact match to its new proposed mark, it takes legal judgment to assess a prior mark that is not exactly the same, but may be 'confusingly similar' to the new mark, and therefore a problem. Consulting a lawyer at the outset will help organizations avoid spending time and money to develop a trademark—such as by buying domain names, hiring a design firm, or creating letterhead—and finding out later that it must be changed."

That being said, there are many examples of similar or identical common law trademarks that coexist without resorting to legal action.

Is there someone on your board who knows this area of the law? That person would be a great resource if you decide you need trademark protection. Law firms often provide a certain amount of pro bono work and may handle trademark filings for you if your nonprofit is small. At any rate, it's important to have a lawyer involved, as this is an area of law that is fairly complex.

Eleven

Looking Inside the Funder's Mind: The Board,
the Staff, and Branding

Your grant has been rejected. Did it have anything to do
with the way you presented your organization (i.e.,
your ineffective brand identity)? That's entirely possible! Grantmakers look long and hard at an organization while deciding whether or not to fund it;
effective branding is, in the broadest sense, a part of
that decision.

Recently, Governance Matters, which you read about
in chapter 9, developed a tool called the "Nonprofit
Governance Indicator Guide: A Funders' Matrix,"
which asks and answers key questions that help clarify
funders' concerns regarding the role governance plays
in creating a sustainable and robust organization. The
answers are written in the voice of the nonprofit. This
insightful interactive tool is for both funders and
nonprofits.

Many of the questions and answers in this tool relate
to brand development in the broadest sense and are
tied together with the important role that the board
and staff play in the development of the organization's
identity. With Governance Matters looking on, I

rewrote a large part of the Funders' Matrix (maintaining the Q&A format) interpreting each question and answer so that it relates more directly to branding.

Unlike nonprofits, big business has made a big investment in branding; for-profits have many of the same branding challenges as nonprofits, just in a different way.

I also illustrated some of the questions and answers with for-profit examples. Why for-profits? Unlike nonprofits, big business has made a big investment in branding; for-profits have many of the same branding challenges as nonprofits, just in a different way. Plus some for-profits have nonprofit arms. The main difference is that for-profits tend to be better equipped to tackle their branding issues. They know solid branding can help them expand, and so they go about branding more aggressively and professionally, whereas nonprofits (which often have tight budgets and depend on volunteer help) may not make growth a top priority. This circumstance poses a conundrum for the nonprofit—to be successful, the nonprofit cannot stagnate, yet it lacks the resources and wherewithal to expand.

Grantmakers' Question: What structures do the members of your staff use to ensure that constituents' needs are understood and addressed?

DK's Interpretation: What research have you done to have an accurate, up-to-date understanding of your audiences? What foundation did you build so that your brand is talking to the people you wish to reach? Is the board aware of how the organization is perceived and is that perception in line with the desired brand identity? Is goodwill seen as a factor?

DK's Answer: We interviewed and studied representative samplings from all audiences prior to branding. When we developed our new Web site/branded materials, we tested them with each audience. Our staff, board, and consultants represent a range of points of view.

One of the biggest errors in judgment nonprofits make is thinking they *are* the audience—that they have an *innate* understanding of their audience. Extensive and ongoing surveying is the only way to understand profoundly whom the organization is serving, and to understand how the organization is perceived.

It is through a range of opinions that true and meaningful innovation may be cultivated. For instance, Apple Computer's board reflects a diversity of thinking: On board are Mickey Drexler, Al Gore, and Steve Jobs. Currently Mickey Drexler is the chairman of J.Crew and he was the marketing genius who put Gap on the fast track. Former Vice President Al Gore is also on the board; his interest in technology and, specifically, the Internet is, of course, famous. Apple's CEO is Steve Jobs (he's also CEO of Pixar, the very high-profile, effectively branded computer/entertainment company), who is the originator of the Apple brand. These are three strong personalities with very developed opinions, yet none of them would make the mistake of second-guessing their audience. And they all have a keen understanding of the value of goodwill—the basis of brand loyalty. All these values get conveyed to the staff, who, of course, are the ultimate implementers of the organization's mission.

The point is that your board (and staff) *should* include strong personalities with developed opinions that are informed by accurate, up-to-date research. The brand is a living, breathing thing that can't grow without the right kind of fuel!

Grantmakers' Question: How do you evaluate the effectiveness and efficiency of your programs and operations?

DK's Interpretation: How do you know you're having the desired impact? How do you know you spend your resources wisely?

DK's Answer: As a nonprofit, our first priority is effective delivery of services in an efficient way that maximizes the use of scarce resources. Our regular annual evaluation of programs and operations determines how successful this has been. The same principle is applied to our organization's image. Efficiency comes from a high return resulting from our branded, response-driven materials, including our Web site. Effectiveness is rated by reactions to our image-driven materials and Web site.

Our staff gathers feedback on our materials (and Web site), which they synthesize and supply to the board.

High efficiency and effectiveness are the result of making a substantial investment in a sound plan—including fundraising materials. A typical rationale for not investing adequately is the expense. Here's a typical nonprofit conundrum: If we have surplus funds, shouldn't it go into programming, not fundraising? While no one wishes to break the bank, here's a truism: The most expensive fundraising tool is the one that doesn't work. Which would you choose: to spend $50,000 to raise $1,000,000 or $5,000 to raise $10,000? Invest wisely.

One efficient approach is to develop a campaign designed to accomplish several things at one time (i.e., promote a program but also fundraise). Whatever you do, consider how you will be able to evaluate the success of the approach so you can replicate and build on it.

Grantmakers' Question: Does the board approve an annual fundraising plan?

DK's Interpretation: Does the board know what it takes to plan for fundraising? Has it acknowledged the need for the creation of comprehensively branded materials that can also be used in fundraising? Does the board (and staff) appreciate the value that good branding and design play in fundraising?

DK's Answer: The board upholds a high standard for the organization: Web site/materials are up to date, comprehensive, transparent, and consistent with our mission and our image, both of which support our fundraising plan.

Our staff creates a powerful, well-designed packet of materials about our programs for each grant proposal. Our Web site has taken into account the fact that funders will scrutinize it.

Frequently, both the board and the staff look at fundraising materials, such as the annual report, too narrowly. Fundraising is an opportunity to go well beyond raising funds: to develop enthusiasm and commitment to the organization with many different audiences, and to develop a clear, credible perception of the organization. This, in turn, raises much more than just funds. Well-branded materials are key to that goal.

Board members also leave the planning to staff or consultants. But silence equals approval, so if the effort fails, the responsibility should be shared.

Grantmakers' Question: Is the board playing an appropriate role in the current stage of the organization's life cycle?

DK's Interpretation: How is your board involved in articulating the brand? In promoting growth? Is your brand positioned to grow as it evolves?

DK's Answer: The board is up to speed about branding and signs off on all major brand-related decisions. Our branding materials, including our Web site, are authoritative, differentiated, and clear because there are professional designers, writers, photographers, and/or marketers involved with each component.

Apple Computer's concern for branding seems obvious; they sell brand-driven products. But Apple's understanding of branding goes much further than any one product: Apple's canny sense of their audiences and their competition has allowed them to become uniquely identified with computer technology and entertainment—making it possible for Apple to expand from the beige Macintosh desktop computers of the 1980s to the nouveau design of the iMacs to white iBooks to the sleekness of iPods of today (and beyond!). The broad, strong family feeling in product design and promotion gives you the sense that you will always know an Apple when you see one.

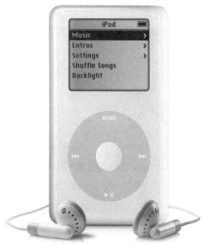

Image 68.
Apple's iPod

How did they do this? Apple hired brand-savvy staff and consultants, listened to marketing, and internalized their lessons. The principle is the same for nonprofits—if the board and staff understand how to use branding with confidence, they can steer the organization to evolve in exciting ways because the organization is communicating transparently and intelligently as it travels through its life cycle. Otherwise, the cycle can become a circle.

Grantmakers' Question: How do board members engage their networks to support the organization's mission?

DK's Interpretation: What branded materials (including your Web site) might board members use to articulate the purposes of the organization to their networks, in order to dialogue with and recruit others?

DK's Answer: Our board actively uses our materials; it was integrally involved in directing our materials and Web site by providing informed feedback and approval at all stages.

We have a board-approved "elevator conversation" that each board and key staff member uses to engage colleagues, strategic partners, and funders in casual conversation about our organization.

Whether at an important meeting or in casual conversation, board members need support in order to engage others—the kind of support that comes with well-designed, well-written, solidly branded materials. All board members need to understand and have confidence in the message of the organization. This seems so obvious! Yet fuzzy branding is the norm in the nonprofit world. Eyes glaze over when board members struggle to explain the mission. And the ripple effect starts from the board. Benjamin Warnke, president of Warnke Community Consulting in New York, warns, "Nonprofits will not get anywhere if they can't learn to clearly say what it is they do." An elevator conversation is more gentle and reasonable than an elevator pitch (since a conversation is much more collaborative than a pitch anyhow—and collaboration is a concept which is part of most nonprofit cultures).

Image 69. The Target image is not what you would expect from a discount store. That's a large part of why its branding works. It's unique

Clear communication builds trust. Did you know that you can access the Target *interactive* annual report from their Web site (*www.target.com*)? And if you scroll down to the bottom of the home page, you'll see a bar with links to community, diversity

Image 70. *The Target dog is part of what makes the branding fun and familiar*

(including employees and suppliers), literature, and investors, as well as to the Target Foundation, which funds arts and social service programs. Access to this information not only makes clear to everyone what and who Target is, but it builds goodwill (which is highly valued), making it clear why Target is loved by so many across economic and sociological lines.

This clarity comes from the Target board (which includes top executives from major popular brands: Pepsi, UPS, Xerox, General Mills, and Orange) and is very attractive to strategic partners and investors. Is your board composition effective?

Lee Green, longtime director of corporate identity and design at IBM, says the board mix must include communicators. He says, "If branding is seen as a highly strategic opportunity or problem area, it would be wise to consider adding experienced professionals to the board who are in a good position to speak to that need."

Governance Matters for Grantmakers adds, "Our board members can accurately identify opportunities to raise the organization's profile in the community. . . . It has a public relations strategy that communicates its message and also attracts support in the community and/or field. Board members can describe the mission and key programs accurately and demonstrate understanding of their competitive advantages and developmental needs."

Grantmakers' Question: Do the organization's programs reflect its structure and functions?

DK's Interpretation: Are the programs consistent with the organization's mission? Do the materials and Web site look and feel like they accurately reflect your organization?

DK's Answer: Everything that goes out is developed and scrutinized to meet the test of brand effectiveness. We have a brand strategy and a brand steward to keep us on track.

Everything from printed and Web materials, office furnishings, and the way our receptionist answers the phone to the way our staff responds to our constituency is a reflection of our organization's brand.

You can always tell when an organization has a strong structure for branding. And that means a brand steward has been empowered by the board to put on the brakes if the train is headed off a cliff or about to take an unscheduled detour. Remember when BP used to be called British Petroleum? It was a programmatic decision to expand beyond fossil fuel to solar and wind energy. But it was a branding decision to change British Petroleum to *Beyond* Petroleum, and they walk the walk. Some BP gas stations now have solar energy panels on their islands, and their logo is an ornate sunflower in green and yellow. The uncharted alternative energy commitment is a risky and brave stance for an energy company to take, but it's one that has thoroughly differentiated BP from all others: Everything either works to build the brand or to defeat it.

Image 71. BP is taking a leadership role in the energy arena— a winning approach for customers

Grantmakers' Question: Does the board actively support efforts to form strategic alliances to maximize client benefit?

DK's Interpretation: How does your brand identity stack up when compared to the organizations you wish to be associated with? Do you consider the branding of those you align your organization with?

DK's Answer: Our strategic partners are a harmonious part of our strong foundation. Our well-designed, state-of-the-art brand differentiates us while highlighting our relevance. We are consistently branded. Our audiences know who we are and why they should care!

It's easy enough to view the home page of those organizations that you would like to make a strategic alliance with. Then compare to your site. (Obviously, this is a bit simplistic—an organization's branding cannot be judged by its Web site alone—but this is a practical way to make comparisons.) Ask yourself how your organization's branding stacks up against theirs. Now look at the sites of your current strategic partners. How do they look next to your organization's? You are known by the company you keep!

To recap:

- The board is key to sound branding.

- Understanding and implementing a solid branding program is essential to funding.

- Getting good, brand-savvy staff and professionals involved in your organization is of paramount importance to branding and funding.

Funding Branding for Nonprofits

I asked Donna Panton, funding consultant to nonprofits and president of Rillbrook Consulting, Inc., an organization development consulting firm in New York City, to answer some direct questions about the funding of branding for nonprofits.

Q: **If they see it as such an important factor in the sustainability of the nonprofit, why don't funders fund branding?**

A: *They will fund branding, but not when it is approached as cosmetics. Tie it into education, and the funder will understand that you are reaching out to your constituency. The recasting of an organization goes much deeper than the design of a logo and, in that context, branding can become a program enhancement, if your new persona and message improve the services you provide.*

Q: **If an organization is re-branding in order to bolster itself, is that fundable?**

A: *Play to your strengths, not to your weaknesses. You won't get funding if you are running from something. You have to approach branding in a positive way. If you're redirecting the branding of the organization, point to the future, not the past.*

Q: **Who funds branding?**

A: *The Foundation Center database is perhaps the best source for leads to funders. It's available online for a small fee and in many public libraries, and at the Foundation Centers in New York, San Francisco, Atlanta, Cleveland, and Washington for free. To find out who might fund branding, use keywords like "outreach," "public relations," "publications," "conferences," "education," "technical assistance," "expansion," "capacity-building," or "sustainable" in the search function.*

Q: **Who funds printing of materials? Who funds consultants?**

A: *Corporations and corporate foundations have been known to fund printing. Ideas That Matter is the annual grant awarded by Sappi (www.sappi.com), which funds pre-press, printing, and paper, but not consultants' fees.*

If funders you have a solid relationship with really like what you're doing, they might be able to dip into discretionary funds. This could include funding of planners, designers, photographers, and other consultants. It's really vital that organizations develop and maintain a good relationship with their funders. They are then more inclined to listen to your more innovative ideas.

Q: **Does the culture of the organization affect funding?**

A: *The culture of an organization is palpable within its walls. That culture is also perceptible to the public through the organization's marketing materials, including its Web site and grant proposals. If you offer a competent, welcoming, compassionate environment with effective programs, then your materials should reflect that, and you hope that your funders will feel assured that money given to you will be well spent.*

Twelve

On the Evolution of Branding: You've Come Such
a Long, Long Way, Baby!

It's shortsighted to think that branding developed in the
early days of industrialization, with the start of packaged, mass-produced products. Yet this is what many
people think. And as a result, branding is associated
with commercialization—and this is a very narrow
view to take, to say the least.

The public also tends to think that branding manipulates, and that attitude breeds animosity and mistrust
within the marketplace. And, although branding is
neutral, indeed, this can be true, since even the earliest consumer products used hidden persuasion—
their agendas ranging from angelic to downright
sinister:

▸ Quakers were thought to be extraordinarily honest
businessmen, so the concept of the religion of
Quakerism was used to convey product integrity.
Customers flocked to brands like Quaker Oats,
Quaker Sugar, and Quaker Oil. (The logo included a
man in a flat black hat, which inevitably identified the
company as Quaker.)

- Harley Procter's religious furor inspired him to name his new white soap "Ivory." Ivory Snow was his spokesperson; "99 44/100 percent pure" was his motto. In fact, America's most popular soap was named from the pulpit, after Psalm 45:8: "All thy garments smell of myrrh and aloes and cassia, out of the ivory palaces whereby they have made thee glad."

With so many horrendous examples of brand manipulation in the public eye, it's not hard to understand why some people think branding is evil.

- Coca-Cola was developed as a nerve tonic by an Atlanta druggist who, blatantly ignoring the addictive powers of the coca leaf, called it an "invigorator of the brain."

- Early ads for the highly addictive Camel cigarettes stated that you could "Smoke as many as you want. They never get on your nerves." And, of course, RJR Tobacco famously went on to use the overtly sexual imagery of Joe Camel to ensnare the most susceptible of future smokers—teenage boys. The general condemnation of the tobacco industry's Joe Camel caused Joe's demise.

- A lawsuit was filed against McDonald's, on behalf of two children in New York, which accused the company of misleading kids about the nutritional value of their burgers and fries. The case is on appeal. It shows the fine line between savvy consumers who are wary of being manipulated for profit and those out to make money from this ignorance. The lawsuit motivated people to file copycat lawsuits and inspired a critically acclaimed independent film called *Super Size Me*, wherein the director/producer/star ate only McDonald's food for a month to ascertain its detrimental effects, which were many, some very serious.

With so many horrendous examples of brand manipulation in the public eye, it's not hard to understand why some people think branding is downright evil; that it promotes decadence and indulgence; that branding is, in and of itself, emblematic of the degeneration of society.

Of course, in the early days, "branding" was not a term—marketing, advertising, or corporate identity were the monikers used. Branding is a relatively new idea in that sense, and it combines all of the above and more. But because branding is often identified with filthy lucre and abuse of power, people often have a negative response to the word itself. They may substitute "spirit" or "style" or some other word for branding to eradicate the stigma. My opinion: it is still branding no matter what you call it.

But branding is simply a tool—and the tendency to brand is inherent in us all, for better or for worse. For every example of manipulative branding, you can find thousands that are straightforward. The Red Cross, ACLU, Campbell Soup, Johnson & Johnson, Amnesty International, Heinz, Ben & Jerry's, the World Wildlife Fund, Neutrogena, the National Geographic Society, HBO, Memorial Sloan-Kettering, Silk Soy products, Oprah, and Jet Blue are just a few of the respected names that rely on branding to make it clear what they offer us, how they enrich, ease, or protect our lives.

As Princeton ethicist and philosopher Kwame Anthony Appiah puts it, "Humans are identity-bearing and identity-creating creatures....It's something we make up. We have to learn to manage it." Identity (or branding) in the broadest sense is a confirmation of who we are. It's a way of establishing individuality. Branding is the systematic way we establish identity for ourselves. And it has always been this way.

The dawn of man: The first tribe was not branded, the second tribe was. In order for the second tribe to distinguish itself from the first, it needed to brand itself. And as soon as the second tribe branded, the first one probably did as well. And it's been that way ever since, especially in America where the competitive advantage is hard won, highly valued.

One of the earliest symbols designed by humans was the wheel of life—what we call the swastika. This symbol is found in many places in the world, notably in India and in the earliest artifacts of the people we ironically call Indians—the first peoples of our land. What fallacious branding! Amerigo Vespucci did not discover America and Columbus did not discover India when he landed here, yet we refer to the people who were here first as American Indians. And, of course, the swastika was famously exploited in the twentieth century in Nazi Germany. From that time on, this very powerful and positive icon has been associated with evil, at least in the Western mind. And so when young Prince Harry of Great Britain wore a Nazi armband to a party in Britain, he was admonished as thoughtless and callous. To wear an armband with a swastika (from a Sanskrit word, *svatika*, meaning well-being, good fortune, luck) in India, however, would, if anything, get you a nod and the salutation "namestae ji," because the swastika is a positive symbol in that part of the world and remains ubiquitous there.

In the East, where religion and magical thinking are powerful, pervasive, interlocked forces, symbols are meant to

Image 72. *Goods carrier from Rajasthan, India, displays a good luck sign, shoe, and devil as protection.* Photograph by DK Holland

protect and alert people. India's peoples are blessed with seemingly boundless creativity, often used to express their complex and imaginative thinking. Goods carriers, the buses that haul people and cargo across the treacherous roads of India and other

Image 73. A goods carrier with the wheel of life on its windshield. Photograph by DK Holland

countries of the region, are adorned with symbols of protection: devils, shoes, wheels of life, birds, lions. The drivers feel these symbols keep the trucks safe as they speed along on rocky, potholed, two-lane highways and negotiate hairpin turns in the mountainous areas (they don't use turn signals—they honk instead). And because the trucks must be taxed as they travel through different regions of India, the design of each fleet of trucks is unique to its district—a practical use of branding.

Brilliant color is a large element in the brand identity of India. That's because many of its religions ascribe specific values to each color in the spectrum: If you are Hindu, on certain days you wear blue, and on others you must never wear white. Nothing is left to

Image 74. A reminder to the drivers behind that their Hindu wives are waiting for them, so they should drive carefully! Photograph by DK Holland

chance. Since many of the religions of India have similar beliefs—Sikhs, Janes, Hindus, Muslims, and Buddhists—each has its own distinctive (branded) dress and color identity to distinguish people by age and gender. And so an extraordinary amount of intense color and colorful symbols dot the landscape as you travel around the country.

Many of the tools Hitler exploited co-opted beauty. Wagner's music and the posters and architecture of the Third Reich were powerful, majestic—and attractive. Beauty attracts.

Hitler co-opted the swastika for his logo. He chose the colors for their meaning—black (revolution), white (national purity), and red (society). He wrote in *Mein Kampf* that "For the future it was unbearable to lack an emblem that had the character of a symbol of the movement and that as such could be put up in opposition to the communists." He added, "The new flag had to be as much a symbol of our own fight as, on the other hand, it had to have an effect as great as that of a poster. . . . In hundreds of thousands of cases, an effective emblem can give the first impetus for the interest in the movement." As abhorrent as Nazi Germany was, the beauty and power of the branding of the Third Reich was and is undeniable.

War Brands

Another use of branding is seen in the uniforms of the military. From the beginning of man, warring factions each had a uniform clearly designed to differentiate its troops from its enemy's, to scare off its foes, to show off its machismo, and to keep its soldiers from being killed (or, if killed, allowing for their bodies to be found).

And the same is true today: Opposing guerrilla armies in America's inner cities—the Bloods and Crips—identify themselves by using red or blue clothing, respectively. How ironically American! They wear bandanas, create unique graffiti in their communities, and tag themselves with tattoos (i.e., logos) to differentiate themselves and their gangs from the others. Would there be a Bloods if there were no Crips?

They play off each other. And, like mirror images, they both chose bandanas, tattoos, and graffiti to represent their brands. And, in turn, this branding provides a sense of community for these inner-city kids, misguided though it may be.

Tibetan Buddhism is a brand in distress, its constituents largely in exile struggling to retain their identity, community, and unique belief system.

Their colors are saffron-orange and red; their spiritual leader is the Dalai Lama. His teachings and the Tibetan Buddhist belief system all model simplicity, compassion, and inward peace. This is their brand.

Image 75. A married Tibetan woman in chupa *and apron.* Photograph by DK Holland

Tibetan girls are branded by one simple and very beautiful dress, a *chupa*. They wear no other styles of clothing. When they marry, they simply add an apron. The lack of choice limits distractions for the Tibetan (a very joyful extroverted people), keeping the focus on the community, inner spirit, not the worldly self.

When China forced the Dalai Lama to flee his homeland in 1959, India invited His Holiness to create Tibet in Exile, in Dharamsala, on the side of a mountain at the foothills of the Himalayas. The Norbulingka Institute was established nearby and houses a complex including temple, nunnery, and monastery—a spiritual community and tourist attraction. It also has a café with authentic Tibetan cuisine and a shop where high-quality classic Tibetan crafts are made and sold all over the world to help preserve the culture of Tibet. A unique color palette and a variety of symbols are part of the branding that distinguishes Tibetan arts and crafts from those of the other cultures of the region.

Confusing the world image of Tibetan Buddhism is the co-option of Tibet by China, which has repopulated Lhasa with Chinese Buddhists loyal to the Chinese government and proclaimed a Chinese Panchen Lama as their spiritual leader. They have also "re-branded" the Tibetan experience by recreating pseudo-authentic and elaborately produced staging of the ancient dance rituals of Tibet.

Most, if not all, religions are branded. The Catholic Church has embraced branding such as the cross, the nuns' habits, and priests' vestments—the amice, alb, cincture, maniple, stole, chasuble, tunicle, dalmatic, cope, buskins, mitre, gallium, succinctorium, and fanon. The rituals, cathedrals, and pope himself are part of the brand. In fact, the Holy See has one of the most magnificent, visually attractive, and sophisticated Web sites on the Internet, which includes virtual visits to the Vatican and a mass led within its walls by the pope, a beautiful and powerful spiritual ritual. Many products come from Vatican City— rosaries, bed sheets, even luggage medals, including a St. Anthony relic medal that contains "a small piece of linen touched to the saint's uncorrupted tongue," recently at auction on eBay.

America is a state of mind, and people from all over the world strive to become part of that mindset. It's one of the largest, most complex brands: the flag—red, white, and blue; the name itself—the United States of America; the architecture of the capital; the songs, monuments, and its folklore; the melting pot; the can-do attitude. They all reinforce the big promises of freedom, happiness, diversity, and respect for the individual: Everything talked about in the Constitution is part of the brand. Sub-brands like California, Texas, and New York reinforce the bigness and boldness of the place.

Image 78. *America the Branded*

If America were to eliminate immigration for political refugees, for instance, the brand promise of "liberty and justice for all" would lose integrity and therefore meaning. If the Constitution—the U.S.A.'s "mission statement"—were compromised, the brand would erode. How well America keeps its brand promise (through the management of its government, corporations, institutions, etc.) defeats or builds its brand.

President George W. Bush, MBA, decided to re-brand the United States in an effort to change the increasingly negative view of America existing beyond its borders. Charlotte Beers, celebrated as the "Queen of Branding" among the public relations cognoscenti, was named Undersecretary of State for Public Diplomacy and Public Affairs three short weeks

Image 79. *What impression does this Web site leave you with?*

after 9/11. Her job was explaining and selling the Bush administration's foreign policy, especially the war on terrorism. "Why do they hate us?" was rephrased, in adspeak, as "How do we reposition the brand?"

To help win market shares from the jihads, Beers, the former chairwoman of the advertising agency, J. Walter Thompson Worldwide, received a $520 million congressional appropriation to focus on "disaffected populations," especially in the Middle East and South Asia. As Beers testified, "a poor perception of the U.S. leads to unrest, and unrest has proven to be a threat to our national and international security." She added that with the U.S.A. brand, as with any great brand, "The leverageable asset is the emotional underpinning of the brand—or what people believe, what they think, how they feel when they use it."

But this contrived idea was met with great mistrust. Plus it was seen as manipulative to put an advertising executive in a government position. Beers's tenure was cut short. She resigned less than two years later.

Coming to Unity

With branding comes a lot of intangible benefits. Early warriors must have felt unstoppable when they camouflaged themselves by putting on war paint and breastplates, dancing in unison as they went off to war. And that sameness or anonymity and volume communicated a sense of threatening power that helped them take on their enemies. (The same clearly would not have been true had they slipped on tutus and colored their lips pink.)

So in that sense, branding becomes a tool for creating unity of purpose. What does communication mean, after all, but community, common, unity?

Tibetan Buddhists, neo-Nazis, the Crips and the Bloods, Catholics, and Americans share common ground in that each is striving to express a common point of view—to communicate to a community and, often, to coalesce a diverse group.

Branding has been a language of persuasion, using clichés and conceits for good and for bad ever since man first walked the Earth. Some of the examples I've included in this chapter were conscious attempts to brand. Some were naturally occurring identities where branding happened automatically, just as ants instinctively create an anthill.

Not only is branding necessary, but it is happening whether you have taken charge of it or not. And if you have competition or opposition, surely they have access to branding as well. Branding, identity, style, marketing—whatever you want to call it—is there to be taken advantage of by everyone, including non-profits, especially nonprofits.

So just do it! You. I'm talking to you!

Branding Resources

Here are more useful tools to help you develop and nurture your nonprofit brand.

Appendix A: The Aish branding guidelines will show you the depth of a brand system, and how to coordinate it in a range of applications without becoming boring or redundant.

Appendix B: "Branding the AIGA" is a document that shows how one organization tackled the issue of getting and keeping its membership engaged in the process of branding.

Appendix C: BAM Graphic Standards Guide

Appendix D: The Governance Matters preliminary presentation presented to its membership for ratification.

The **Brand Glossary** contains all the words and phrases you will need to know in order to communicate about branding.

Additional resources may be found on my Web site, *www.dkholland.com.*

Appendix A

Aish Branding Guide—"Guidelines Without the Guilt"

Author: Lynn Altman,
Viverito + Altman
Brandmaker Express.
Design: Bernhardt
Fudyma Design
Group

Resources

The Quark templates (for Mac platforms only)

Templates:
Aish_palmcard_50/50.qxt
Aish_palmcard_1/3-2/3.qxt
Aish_palmcard_all-type.qxt

Aish_postcard_50/50.qxt
Aish_postcard_1/3-2/3.qxt
Aish_postcard_all-type.qxt

Aish_folded_flyer_50/50.qxt
Aish_folded_flyer_1/3-2/3.qxt

Aish_flat_flyer_50/50.qxt
Aish_flat_flyer_1/3-2/3.qxt

Contact the following people with any questions or for guidance in the production of all advertising, direct mail or other promotion materials.

Shayna Goldsmith	Adam Jacobs	Rabbi Elazar Grunberger	Talia Edgar
313 West 83rd Street	313 West 83rd Street	8149 Delmar Boulevard	7717 Gannon #2E
New York, NY 10024	New York, NY 10024	St Louis, MO 63130	St Louis, MO 63130
212-579-1388 ext.33	212-579-1388 ext.25	314-862-2474	314-725-2663
sgoldsmith@aish.com	ajacobs@aish.com	egrunberger@aish.com	tedgar@aish.com

Images

Reasonably priced stock photographs are available form various sources. Some stock photography houses even offer collections of images on disc ('royalty-free' only) as well as single images.

Please note that if you purchase a 'rights-managed' image you will ONLY be able to use the image in the single piece that you have bought those rights to use it in. And you can only use it one time. Any other usage of that image will require that you obtain additional rights for that image with the company that you purchased it from. Please consult with the company when purchasing the image to learn about the rights you are buying as each company is different.

However, most stock image companies do have 'royalty-free' images that they sell. What does this mean? It means that when you purchase a 'royalty-free' image you can use it as often as you like on as many pieces as you like without having to pay additional fees. Again, please consult with the company when purchasing the image to learn about the rights you are buying as each company is different.

Some stock companies to check out (these are a few of many):
www.gettyone.com
www.veer.com
www.masterfile.com
www.corbis.com
www.photonica.com
www.nonstock.com
www.agefotostock.com

Font

The Profile font can be purchased online at **www.fontfont.com** with Mac and PC versions available. Make sure you purchase the correct version as the PC fonts will not work on Macs and vice-versa. For pricing and policies please review company website.

33

Introduction

Contents

As Aish's membership, branches and offerings continue to grow and our communication efforts increase, it is important to maintain a clearly focused identity and "personality" in our various advertising, direct mail and announcement vehicles. By adhering to a visually cohesive set of graphic and copy guidelines we will present a consistent imprimatur that will not only increase recognition of our name and offerings, but also, over time, will become synonymous with our reputation for providing entertaining, interesting and meaningful programs for the Jewish community.

The identity system outlined on the following pages introduces the overall brand attributes and explains their characteristics, interrelationships and applications. It is based on a clean, open and minimalist page layout and a distinctive voice. Although the elements on the page are consistently organized, there is ample creative elbow room to allow the creation of all manner of Aish communications.

These guidelines are structured in four sections:

– In the first section, the five key brand attributes are introduced, with examples of the visual characteristics and discussion of the desired tone and "attitude" for headlines and copy.

– Then, in the second section, everything is put together in various combinations to show how materials of all kinds can be produced.

– The third section is a brief description of logo variations and which ones to use in different printing situations.

– And finally, a sampling of "makeovers" that uses actual Aish materials and shows how they would/could look if they had been designed within the new branding guidelines.

These guidelines provide the needed specifications to enable the many Aish personnel responsible for the creation of our communications to apply the proper formatting, style and "attitude" to all of the materials that we produce in the future.

2

Brand attributes

The five major building blocks of Aish's new identity are:

The underlying grid/page architecture.
The characteristics/handling of imagery.
The Profile font.
The color palette(s).
Headline/Copy tone.

These attributes are explained in more depth on the following pages, and, as you will see, although they are well defined, they all have options that provide the flexibility needed to accommodate different types of components, structures, varying content and amounts of copy, different styles of imagery and varying printing requirements.

Even with this high degree of flexibility, if applied properly, the various combinations of these attributes will result in a consistent "look-and-feel" for all manner of Aish communications.

*Rectangular and silhouette image styles are used exclusively with specific page architectures. More detailed specifications about imagery usage appear on page 5.

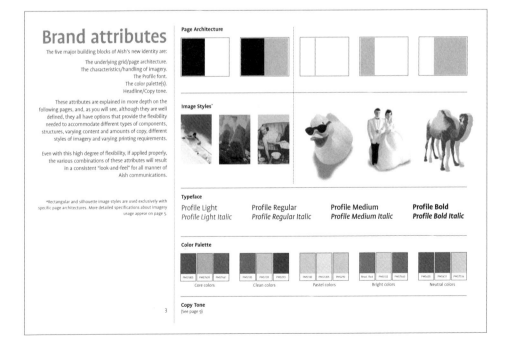

Page Architecture

Image Styles*

Typeface

Profile Light
Profile Light Italic

Profile Regular
Profile Regular Italic

Profile Medium
Profile Medium Italic

Profile Bold
Profile Bold Italic

Color Palette

Core colors   Clean colors   Pastel colors   Bright colors   Neutral colors

Copy Tone
(See page 9)

3

Page architecture

Most single page items (flyers, bulletin board announcements, postcards* and palmcards) are composed in a landscape orientation.

The two optional page configurations, both divide the page on the horizontal axis, one at the mid-point, the other into a 1/3 - 2/3 proportion. Each configuration has different possibilities for the application of imagery and background colors:

When using the mid-point (50/50) axis, the left half of the page *always* contains a rectangular image, with the right half featuring the headline and all other message copy.** When using the 1/3 - 2/3 axis, a silhouette image Is always used. The Image also spans the line between the two portions of the page to some degree. This configuration can be used with either size field on the left or right, with a completely white background, or with a color field in either one of the two fields.***

Also note that all flyer/mailer type component templates have been designed with an intentional, consistent, 1/4-inch white border so that they can be reproduced on most conventional laser printers that don't print to the edge of the page. If you are printing any item with a professional printer, you can "bleed" the images and color fields if desired.

*Text only postcards are held vertically for the front. (See page 12 for details)

50/50 Configuration

**The right half of a 50/50 configuration can retain a white background, or apply a color to that field.

1/3 - 2/3 Configuration

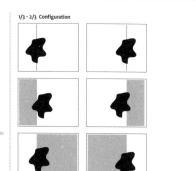

*** When using a color in either field, the edge of that color field automatically delineates the 1/3 - 2/3 proportion. However, when using a totally white background, the proportion must be indicated with a rule (see rule specs on page 10).

4

Imagery

Again, depending on the page configuration chosen, the image used will be either a rectangular contained image (for 50/50 pages) or a free-floating silhouetted image (for 1/3 - 2/3 pages).

Either type of image can be handled in a variety of styles:

Rectangular images can be full color, a black halftone* over a solid color background or a color halftone over a second color background. (See figures 1, 2 and 3;)

Silhouette images can also be full color or black and white halftones (figures 4 and 5). In addition, there is a style for silhouettes that manipulates the original photo by varying degrees to create a more high contrast, grainier and/or multiple exposed image.** (Figures 6, 7 and 8.)

*A halftone is an image reproduced in its full tonal range in a single color.

**This technique requires a knowledge of Photoshop or other software with image manipulation capabilities. it is a good way to overcome pictures of poor quality or make images of different styles consistent.

Rectangular Images **Silhouetted Images**

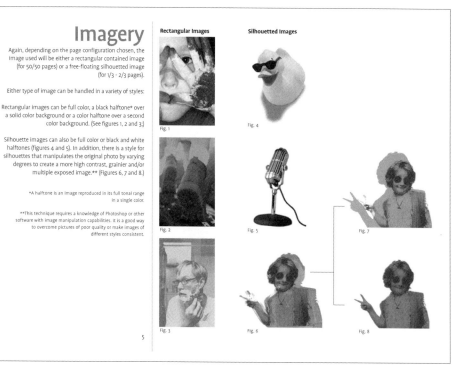

Fig. 1

Fig. 4

Fig. 2

Fig. 5

Fig. 7

Fig. 3

Fig. 6

Fig. 8

5

Typefaces

There is only one font used for all text/copy elements.

That font is **Profile.**

The font can be used in any of the weights and/or italics shown at the right.

In all but the smallest point sizes, text is always negatively tracked or tightly kerned and leaded. *

Most samples in this document, the font display at the right and all page headings are tracked (kerned) a minimum of -4, with certain letter pairs kerned even tighter. The degree of negative leading is based on the particular arrangement of ascending and descending letters - or the lack thereof.

Holy rollers wanted.	Holy rollers wanted.	Holy rollers wanted.
normal kern auto leading	negative kerning auto leading	negative kerning negative leading

* Kerning/tracking is the adjustment of the spaces between individual letters or words. Leading is the space between lines of text.

There is no set formula for the degree of kerning and leading, but rather it is based on the overall visual characteristics of the individual headline, letter pairs, the size of the component and the ability to do so in any given situation.

Punctuation (including quotes, commas, etc.) should also be kerned as necessary.

If ellipses are needed, they should be created by using 3 individual periods which can also be kerned tighter.

Profile Light
Profile Light Italic

Profile Regular
Profile Regular Italic

Profile Medium
Profile Medium Italic

Profile Bold
Profile Bold Italic

The Profile font can be purchased online at **www.fontfont.com** with Mac and PC versions available. Make sure you purchase the correct version as the PC fonts will not work on Macs and vice-versa. For pricing and policies please review company website.

6

Color palette

There are twelve colors in the core palette. They have been chosen to help maintain consistency while providing sufficient variation to compliment most possible imagery and have other appropriate usages based on the season or a specific event.

The 12 colors in the core palette consist of the three primary colors (red, yellow and blue), the three secondary colors (orange, green and violet) and the six tertiary colors. The chart at the right gives both the Pantone match colors and the four-color equivalent for each.

These core colors are of a more sophisticated nature. Therefore, we have also developed ancillary palettes (for the primary and secondary colors only) that may be more suitable for communications with different constituencies (such as college students or children) or about certain types of events (such as a comedy night, a mother/child pottery painting class or a '70s theme party).

Those ancillary palettes, and an additional selection of neutral colors, are displayed on the following page.

PLEASE NOTE that due to the differences of color printers and monitors, color should be determined only by using a printed Pantone PMS/CMYK swatch book and not by their appearance when viewing them on a screen or printed by a desktop color printer.

PMS 7409 C0M30Y95K0 — Yellow
PMS 138 C0M38Y94K0
PMS 584 C12M0Y79K6
PMS 717 C0M51Y100K6 — Orange
PMS 370 C60M0Y100K28 — Green
PMS 7417 C0M75Y75K0
PMS 320 C100M0Y31K6
PMS 1805 C0M91Y100K24 — Red
PMS 7461 C78M28Y0K0 — Blue
PMS 682 C28M76Y0K6
PMS 7456 C55M35Y0K7
Violet
PMS 668 C69M65Y0K30

7

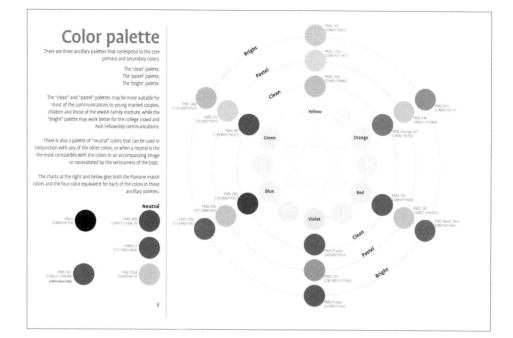

Color palette

There are three ancillary palettes that correspond to the core primary and secondary colors:

The 'clean' palette.
The 'pastel' palette.
The 'bright' palette.

The "clean" and "pastel" palettes may be more suitable for most of the communications to young married couples, children and those of the Jewish Family Institute, while the "bright" palette may work better for the college crowd and Aish Fellowship communications.

There is also a palette of "neutral" colors that can be used in conjunction with any of the other colors, or when a neutral is the most compatible with the colors in an accompanying image or necessitated by the seriousness of the topic.

The charts at the right and below give both the Pantone match colors and the four-color equivalent for each of the colors in these ancillary palettes.

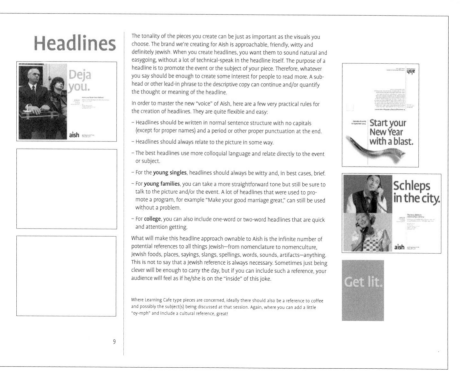

Headlines

The tonality of the pieces you create can be just as important as the visuals you choose. The brand we're creating for Aish is approachable, friendly, witty and definitely Jewish. When you create headlines, you want them to sound natural and easygoing, without a lot of technical-speak in the headline itself. The purpose of a headline is to promote the event or the subject of your piece. Therefore, whatever you say should be enough to create some interest for people to read more. A sub-head or other lead-in phrase to the descriptive copy can continue and/or quantify the thought or meaning of the headline.

In order to master the new "voice" of Aish, here are a few very practical rules for the creation of headlines. They are quite flexible and easy:

– Headlines should be written in normal sentence structure with no capitals (except for proper names) and a period or other proper punctuation at the end.

– Headlines should always relate to the picture in some way.

– The best headlines use more colloquial language and relate directly to the event or subject.

– For the **young singles**, headlines should always be witty and, in best cases, brief.

– For **young families**, you can take a more straightforward tone but still be sure to talk to the picture and/or the event. A lot of headlines that were used to promote a program, for example "Make your good marriage great," can still be used without a problem.

– For **college**, you can also include one-word or two-word headlines that are quick and attention getting.

What will make this headline approach ownable to Aish is the infinite number of potential references to all things Jewish—from nomenclature to nomenculture, Jewish foods, places, sayings, slangs, spellings, words, sounds, artifacts—anything. This is not to say that a Jewish reference is always necessary. Sometimes just being clever will be enough to carry the day, but if you can include such a reference, your audience will feel as if he/she is on the "inside" of this joke.

Where Learning Cafe type pieces are concerned, ideally there should also be a reference to coffee and possibly the subject(s) being discussed at that session. Again, where you can add a little "oy-mph" and include a cultural reference, great!

The look and feel

Again, Aish's new identity is based on a clean, open and minimalist page layout. The elements on the page are consistently organized and arranged depending on the type of component being produced, the amount/composition of the content and the chosen page architecture.

There are usually only four types of elements: The headline, the image(s), the necessary descriptive text and the logo/tagline signature. (Additional information on these elements are described elsewhere in this document.) There are never any additional borders, boxes, shapes or graphics.*

Copy field backgrounds are either white or one of the Aish palette colors and headlines are always one of the palette colors or a value thereof. Body copy and other descriptive text is predominantly black, but color may be used when needed for emphasis, clarity or differentiation.

*The interiors of some communications may need such elements to help organize complex material. See the Aish New York 'Learning Cafe' materials shown on page 13 as an example.

Flyer

Postcard front   Postcard back   Palmcard

10

The look and feel

All headlines are set in Profile Medium. Although there is an ideal point size for flyers (see next page), most components will be set in point sizes that allow for the largest possible headline depending on its overall length, line breaks or the length of its longest word. (Never hyphenate a word in a headline.)

For headlines that run more than one line, leading will also vary depending on the particular combination of words and the arrangement of their ascenders and descenders. In general, leading should be as tight as possible to make the overall copy block visually even and balanced.*

Contrast among the various text elements is also an important factor. No two adjacent copy elements should be only slightly different in size, color or weight from one another.

All headlines and text are set flush left or right, against either the edge of the page, the edge of a photo or a vertical line. This is a critical part of the identity system.**

*See page 6 for a showing of all weights and styles of the Profile font and a further explanation of leading.

** The vertical line (rule) that appears somewhere on all components is always 1/2 point in weight and always prints in the same color as the headline that accompanies it on the page. (On the back side of post-cards or other one-color surfaces, the rule - and any other text/image element, prints black.) This rule varies in length (height) based on the volume of text that it accompanies and/or amount of space available below the headline to accommodate it.

Flyer

Postcard front   Palmcard

11

Flyers

Flyers are always 8.5" x 11" and are usually composed in a horizontal (landscape) format.* Although each flyer will have its own unique image, headline, color and volume of text, the templates provided for these – and all other basic components – are pre-set with the underlying page grid, fonts and other elements that can simply be modified as necessary.

The ideal point size for the headline text is 112 point, but, depending on the longest word in your headline, it may be necessary to use a slightly smaller point size in order to avoid having to hyphenate a word.

Headlines can be of varying numbers of lines but should always start 3/4 inch from the top of the page. Also, the vertical rule and the subhead or first line of message text should always be 1/2 inch from the bottom of the last line of the headline.

Subtitles are set 16 point using Profile Regular. Most descriptive text is Profile Light (10 point on 12 points of leading), with other weights, italics and or color for highlight or emphasis as needed.

The date, time, location and cost text is set in 8 point on 10 points of leading.

Hint: Use emphasis sparingly, as too many points of emphasis results in a busy page with nothing really being emphasized.

*In certain circumstances, a flyer may be intended to be a self mailer rather than a flat handout. (See the 'Learning Cafe' materials on page 14 for more specifics.)

Folded Flyer

For flat flyers, use QuarkXpress template:
Aish_flat_flyer_50/50.qxt
Aish_flat_flyer_1/3-2/3.qxt

For folded flyers, use QuarkXpress template:
Aish_folded_flyer_50/50.qxt
Aish_folded_flyer_1/3-2/3.qxt

12

Postcards and Palmcards

Postcards and palmcards can be produced in either a vertical or horizontal orientation.

Postcards are always 5" x 7" and palmcards always 4" x 3".

When either uses a headline only (with no imagery),* they are composed in a vertical (portrait) orientation on the front but with a traditional horizontal orientation on the back. In such cases, the front prints in one of the palette colors (as a full bleed background color) and uses a 30% tint of that same color for the headline. The back side prints in black only – unless the flame in the Aish logo is to be red. (See page 19 for specifics on the logo printing.)

When either size card uses an image and a headline, they are designed with a horizontal orientation and can use any page architecture or appropriate variation of imagery style. Again, the back side can print one or two colors.

* Only postcards and palmcards can be produced without imagery, and can rely on the cleverness of the headline to attract attention.

For 5"x7" postcards, use QuarkXpress template:
Aish_postcard_50/50.qxt
Aish_postcard_1/3-2/3.qxt
Aish_postcard_all-type.qxt

For 4"x3" cards, use QuarkXpress template:
Aish_palmcard_50/50.qxt
Aish_palmcard_1/3-2/3.qxt
Aish_palmcard_all-type.qxt

13

The Learning Cafe

Materials produced to promote the Learning Cafe or other similar events always use a unique color to help identify them. This color is part of the neutral palette: Pantone 161 – or its 4 color equivalent (C0M52Y100K64). This color is used exclusively on Learning Cafe materials. All other grid, font, image and copy tone rules for a flyer remain the same.

Exclusive color for Learning Cafe

PMS 161
C0M52Y100K64

Fold

5.5"

8.5"

Folded, self mailing flyers are a special situation. Although they are the same 8.5" x 11" proportion as a regular flat flyer, they are created in a vertical orientation and, when folded, resemble a postcard on the outside.

The detailed information that appears on the inside also has a set format and grid that utilizes additional graphic elements such as color tint areas to help organize information and the silhouetted coffee cup image.

For flat flyers, use QuarkXpress template:
Aish_flat_flyer_50/50.qxt
Aish_flat_flyer_1/3-2/3.qxt
For folded flyers, use QuarkXpress template:
Aish_folded_flyer_50/50.qxt
Aish_folded_flyer_1/3-2/3.qxt

Flat Flyer

Flat Flyer

Folded Flyer

Inside Folded Flyer

14

Invitations

Invitations have a folded size the same as that of a postcard (5" x 7") but can have as many open panels as necessary to accommodate the required content. If more than a simple/single fold, all invitations utilize a 'roll fold' structure to reveal additional information.

Since there are numerous possible horizontal dimensions for invitations, a single template is not possible. Therefore, invitations will have to be constructed from scratch within QuarkXpress.

Remember: When utilizing a gate fold or roll fold structure, each panel after the first two must be made successively smaller by 1/16" to allow it to fold inside the previous one.

A. Simple Fold (5" x 7" when folded, 10" x 7" flat).

B. Gate Fold (5" x 7" when folded, 14 and 15/16" x 7" flat).

C. Roll Fold (5" x 7" folded, ?" x 7" flat).
The length of roll fold structures will vary depending upon how many panels you need.

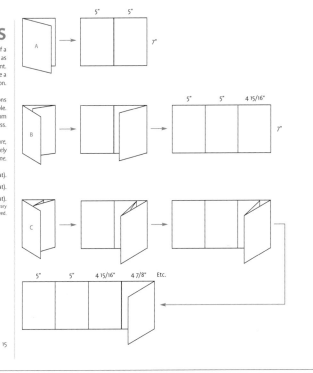

15

Invitations

Headlines (and images) should be developed to take advantage of the roll fold structure.

In this case the roll fold reveals picture/headline pairs.

Unfolded inside

Unfolded outside

16

Invitations

Headlines (and images) should also be developed to take advantage of the roll fold structure.

In this case the roll fold reveals the headline.

Unfolded inside

Unfolded outside

17

Transit Panels

Advertising

As with most other components, ads should be created with image and headline pairs. A single image/headline could be a horizontal 1/2 page ad or a double-page spread in a standard publication format. A sequence of image/headline pairs could be used for transit advertising in buses, subways or cab tops.

Since each advertising situation will have different size/proportion requirements, you must adapt the general look and feel accordingly. Therefore, no templates have been created for advertising, but all other font, color and design specs remain the same.

2 page spread ads

Half page ad

Half page ad

Poster

18

The Signature

The Aish logo, the tagline and the website URL make up the sign-off that appears at the bottom of all advertising and promotion materials.

The elements of the signature are always in a fixed size ratio and relative position to one another. As you will see in the examples used throughout this document, the signature is always placed in combination with the line at the bottom of the page.

The logo has been created as a single piece of electronic art that can be easily scaled to fit materials of various sizes.

The standard version of the logo used a flame that must be created using four-color process printing. When doing so, use this version. However, there is a version with a simplified flame icon that can be printed in a single red color when there is no need (or budget) for four-color printing. That single red color is PMS 1805.

There is also a version of the logo that replaces the flame with a coffee bean for all Learning Cafe type materials or a heart for Jewish Family Institute materials.

aish | Igniting Jewish Pride
www.aish.com

4 Color Process
(For printing full color)

aish | Igniting Jewish Pride
www.aish.com

Greyscale
(For printing in Black only)

| Igniting Jewish Pride
www.aish.com

Two Color
(Use greyscale art, but print flame in PMS 1805)

aish | Igniting Jewish Pride
www.aish.com

4 Color Process
(For printing full color)

aish | Igniting Jewish Pride
www.aish.com

Two Color
(Use greyscale art, but print heart in PMS 1805)

aish
Philadelphia | Igniting Jewish Pride
www.aish.com

19

Makeovers

The following pages feature actual materials previously produced by Aish that, if they had been produced within the new graphic standards, illustrate how they would reinforce a consistent and strong brand identity.

PLEASE NOTE: The makeovers are not actual new materials in use, but rather "hypothetical" illustrations to show how current communications could be executed using the brand attributes.

After

Before

20

Before **After**

21

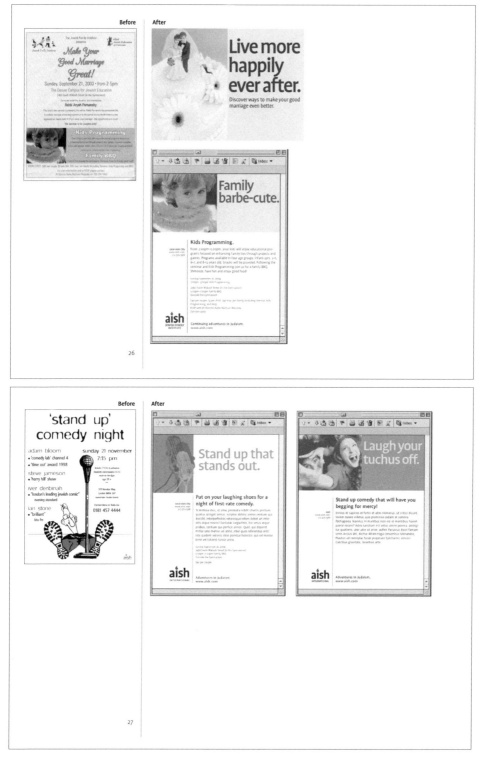

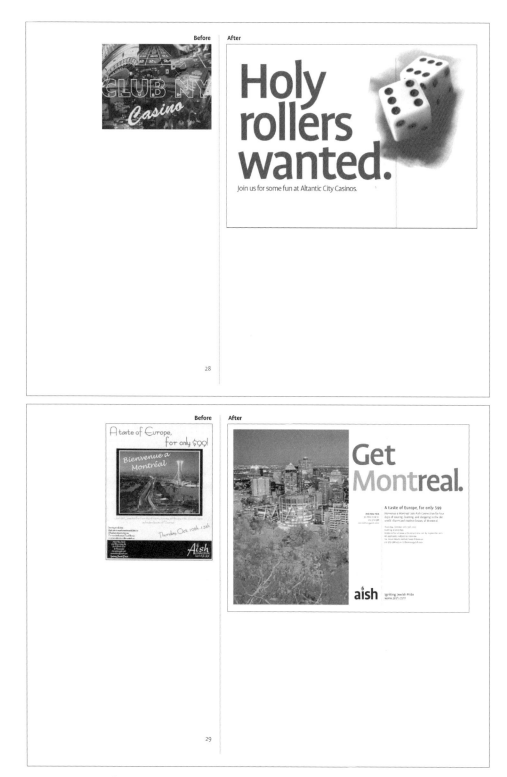

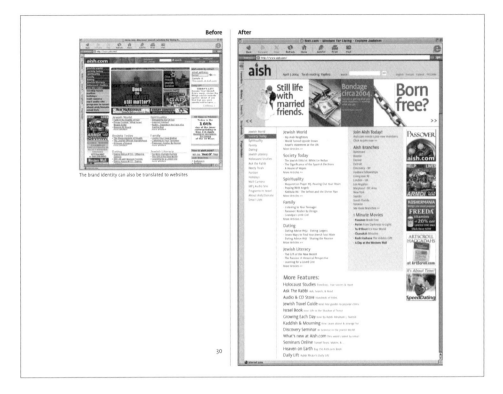

The brand identity can also be translated to websites

30

Before

After

32

Resources

The Quark templates (for Mac platforms only)

Templates:
Aish_palmcard_50/50.qxt
Aish_palmcard_1/3-2/3.qxt
Aish_palmcard_all-type.qxt

Aish_postcard_50/50.qxt
Aish_postcard_1/3-2/3.qxt
Aish_postcard_all-type.qxt

Aish_folded_flyer_50/50.qxt
Aish_folded_flyer_1/3-2/3.qxt

Aish_flat_flyer_50/50.qxt
Aish_flat_flyer_1/3-2/3.qxt

Contact the following people with any questions or for guidance in the production of all advertising, direct mail or other promotion materials.

Shayna Goldsmith
313 West 83rd Street
New York, NY 10024
212-579-1388 ext.33
sgoldsmith@aish.com

Adam Jacobs
313 West 83rd Street
New York, NY 10024
212-579-1388 ext.25
ajacobs@aish.com

Rabbi Elazar Grunberger
8149 Delmar Boulevard
St Louis, MO 63130
314-862-2474
egrunberger@aish.com

Talia Edgar
7717 Gannon #2E
St Louis, MO 63130
314-725-2663
tedgar@aish.com

Images

Reasonably priced stock photographs are available form various sources. Some stock photography houses even offer collections of images on disc ('royalty-free' only) as well as single images.

Please note that if you purchase a 'rights-managed' image you will ONLY be able to use the image in the single piece that you have bought those rights to use it in. And you can only use it one time. Any other usage of that image will require that you obtain additional rights for that image with the company that you purchased it from. Please consult with the company when purchasing the image to learn about the rights you are buying as each company is different.

However, most stock image companies do have 'royalty-free' images that they sell. What does this mean? It means that when you purchase a 'royalty-free' image you can use it as often as you like on as many pieces as you like without having to pay additional fees. Again, please consult with the company when purchasing the image to learn about the rights you are buying as each company is different.

Some stock companies to check out (these are a few of many):
www.gettyone.com
www.veer.com
www.masterfile.com
www.corbis.com
www.photonica.com
www.nonstock.com
www.agefotostock.com

Font

The Profile font can be purchased online at **www.fontfont.com** with Mac and PC versions available. Make sure you purchase the correct version as the PC fonts will not work on Macs and vice-versa. For pricing and policies please review company website.

33

Appendix B

Branding the AIGA

Branding the AIGA.
Why, what, and how.

Draft for Discussion
Third draft, October 13, 1998
Bart Crosby, Crosby Associates Inc.

Why worry?

Whether or not we want to be, we are a brand.

We're out there — people will form opinions about us.
Those opinions will be positive, negative, or ambiguous.
They're probably not going to be neutral.

We're going to be visible or invisible.
We'll get credit for the things we do, or we'll continue to do things and not get credit.
We'll be either understood or misunderstood.

We can be either a good brand or a bad brand;
a clear brand or a confusing brand; a helpful brand or an irritating brand;
a responsible brand or an irresponsible brand.

Why is it important to build a strong, appropriate, consistent AIGA brand?

To attract new members.

To retain the members we have.

To build greater public awareness of and respect for design.

To promote the value of professional graphic design.

To gain greater financial support for the organization.

To gain greater political clout.

What is branding?

Branding is 1) determining who we are, who we serve, and who we influence, 2) determining who we wish to be, serve, and influence, 3) defining the attributes that communicate who we are to our various audiences, and 4) creating a plan for, and managing the communication of those attributes.

Branding defines and establishes the appropriate personality for an organization, product, service, environment, or initiative, and manages the ways in which that personification is communicated.

It is an activity that combines visual identification with desired attributes — activates them, visualizes them, communicates them, and monitors them in order to create the appropriate emotional response from the reader, user, experiencer, or passer-by.

A Brand becomes the personification of an organization, a product, a service, an activity, or an environment. It takes on the characteristics of a person — it can be handsome or homely, smart or dull, well dressed or dowdy, hard working or lazy, clear or confusing, consistent or schizophrenic.

Is our logo our brand?

Our logo represents our organization — it identifies us on things and in places. In and of itself, it doesn't say a whole lot about graphic design, but the more it's connected with high-quality graphic design, the more it becomes representative of high-quality graphic design.

A logotype, or an identifier, is a thing. By itself, it may or may not tell us something about the owner — what they make, what they sell, or what services they offer. As beautiful or unique as a logo may be, it is essentially inanimate. Without an environment — without being placed onto or into something — it has very little to say.

Branding starts when the identifier is placed into an environment.

Placed into positive environments that reflect the goals, values, and initiatives of the organization, our logo will reflect well on the organization and will hopefully deliver the desired messages. Placed into a poor or inappropriate environment, it may misrepresent or confuse our goals, values, and initiatives and reflect negatively on the organization.

Conversely, an environment, an action, a product, or a service may be spectacular, but without an identifier it affords little credit for its owner, producer, or initiator.

Our visual **identity** (or logo) identifies us. It says who we are.

Our **brand** is the activation of our identity, mission, and values. It demonstrates who we are.

The purpose of branding is to evoke an emotional response by embodying the emotional characteristics of the organization within all our messages and actions.

2

It means presenting the AIGA persona consistently, appropriately, and prolifically, in order to ensure that we always get credit for what we are, what we represent, and what we do.

It is the spirit of the organization embedded within every action, communication, product, service, environment, or initiative.

What's the difference between National Branding and Chapter Branding?

There is no difference.

We are the same organization, we have the same members,
we have the same mission and initiatives,
we have the same logo, we have most of the same audiences.

While individual chapters should be identified on, and receive credit for their initiatives, the identity and the presentation of our brand should be philosophically the same.

Who are we?

We've already determined who we are and what we represent:

We are an organization whose purpose is to advance excellence in graphic design as a discipline, profession, and cultural force.

We provide leadership in the exchange of ideas and information, the encouragement of critical analysis and research, and the advancement of education and ethical practice.

We will promote dialogue and strong ties between graphic designers and the business community.

We will become a primary information resource for the history of graphic design.

We will sponsor actions and programs that encourage educational institutions to improve and update the quality of design education in America.

We will promote education and actions that protect the planet from further ecological damage.

We will advance the exchange of ideas and information to increase awareness within the profession of diverse international perspectives about design, culture, and economics.

We will promote understanding of how new technologies are affecting the profession.

We will promote professional practice among graphic designers and provide a forum for discussing values and practices.

We will encourage the graphic design profession's involvement in public service.

3

Who are our audiences?

Our audiences are:
our members
potential members
the business community
academic institutions
educators
students
governments and communities
sponsors and benefactors
potential sponsors and benefactors
allied organizations
the public in general

In most cases, we are "speaking" to multiple audiences.

All of our communications must speak in "languages" that are understood by all of the audiences to whom we are communicating.

How do we do it?

The key to successfully branding AIGA is individual responsibility.

All those involved in creating AIGA communications, environments, and initiatives — designers, writers, the creators of products or services, the editors, the proofreaders — must be personally responsible for ensuring that the attributes of the organization are embodied in every effort; that the audiences are being well served; that the organization is getting credit for all its efforts.

This can't be accomplished with an identity manual or systematic branding guidelines.

It can only be achieved by thoughtful, intelligent, creative efforts by thoughtful, intelligent, creative people who:

1) understand the organization, its mission, its initiatives, its values;

2) understand what needs to be communicated;

3) understand why it's being communicated;

4) know the audiences and what "languages" they speak;

5) and, identify AIGA (using our logo) prominently. (Prominent doesn't mean dominant. It means that it will be seen and recognized without an effort on the viewer's part.)

4

We must program, write, design, and deliver all that we do according to who we say we are.

We must ensure that we are credited for all we do by clearly identifying AIGA and, when appropriate, the local chapter on everything we produce, every service we offer, every initiative we initiate, every environment we create.

What are the tools?

Our name,

our mission, initiatives, and values,

our visual identifier,

and the talents, understanding, and hard work of the people who create, administer, service, design, write, edit, govern, and deliver all that we do.

5

Appendix C

BAM Graphic Standards Guide

Brief but complete guidelines written to introduce and instruct designers to the typographic identity system begun with the 1995 Next Wave Brochure. Creative Direction and Design: Michael Bierut, Pentagram.

Brooklyn
Academy
of
Music

Graphic

Identity

Guidelin

The BAM identifier for
non-corporate publications

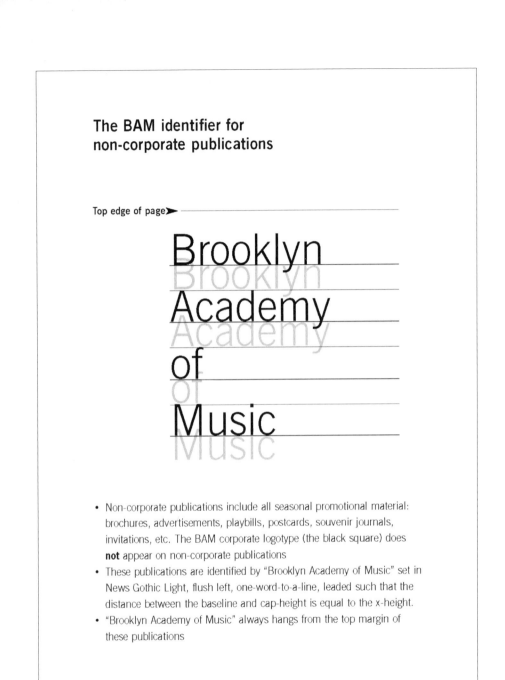

Top edge of page➤

Brooklyn
Academy
of
Music

- Non-corporate publications include all seasonal promotional material: brochures, advertisements, playbills, postcards, souvenir journals, invitations, etc. The BAM corporate logotype (the black square) does **not** appear on non-corporate publications
- These publications are identified by "Brooklyn Academy of Music" set in News Gothic Light, flush left, one-word-to-a-line, leaded such that the distance between the baseline and cap-height is equal to the x-height.
- "Brooklyn Academy of Music" always hangs from the top margin of these publications

The BAM typeface:
News Gothic

News Gothic Light

ABCDFGHIJKLMNOP
QRSTUVWXYZ
abcdefghijklmnopqrstuvwxyz
abcdefghijklmnopqrstuvwxyz

News Gothic Roman

ABCDFGHIJKLMNOP
QRSTUVWXYZ
abcdefghijklmnopqrstuvwxyz
abcdefghijklmnopqrstuvwxyz

News Gothic Bold

**ABCDFGHIJKLMNOP
QRSTUVWXYZ
abcdefghijklmnopqrstuvwxyz
*abcdefghijklmnopqrstuvwxyz***

- Headlines and large type are set in News Gothic Light.
- Avoid all caps
- News Gothic Bold is used for subheads only and should not be used above 13pt, except on large format items like posters.
- The optimum size and leading for text set in News Gothic is 8/12
- Text is set in News Gothic Light except when reversed out of black or another color, in which case News Gothic Roman is substituted.
- In text-heavy publications—annual reports, souvenir books, magazine-style brochures, etc.—a second typeface is permissible. Bembo has been identified and employed as one such second typeface.

Relationship between the BAM logotype and the surrounding type

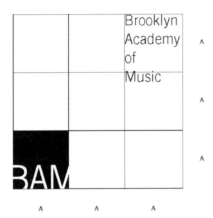

- In most cases the logo will butt up to the left-hand margin of the publication.
- The size of the logo can usually be established as half a column-width of the publication (in this case, the column-width would be 2 x A). This rule places "Brooklyn Academy of Music" at the top of the second column
- The logo is placed at a distance from the top margin that is twice its height
- Where it is used as a title or identifying device, rather than in continuous prose, "Brooklyn Academy of Music" is set one-word-to-a-line and in a size such that the longest word, "Academy", is aproximately the same width as the logo
- "Brooklyn Academy of Music" is positioned hanging from the top margin and at a distance to the right of the logo equal to the logo's width.
- The leading of "Brooklyn Academy of Music" is established so that the x-height of "Music" sits at a distance from the top margin that is equal to the height of the logo

The BAM titling type style

Orlando

Next Wave

- The BAM titling typestyle is achieved by truncating the type on one, two, three or all four sides using a black or colored bar, the edge of a page, or simply an imagined line. Legibility must be maintained by carefully judging the portion of the characters left showing.
- Titles are set in News Gothic Light and should be tightly spaced. The type should be kerned at least 2–5 points overall depending on point size (more in larger sizes) and then individual character and word-spacing should be modified where necessary for general evenness.
- An impression of spatial depth is created in part by dramatically varying the point size of the titling type, from word to word, or phrase to phrase.
- Conceal the ends of rounded lower-case characters like "e", "a", "s" and "c", either by cutting them off at a point just above or below the end of the stroke, or by masking them.

The Duchess

of Malfi

Appendix D

Governance Matters Presentation

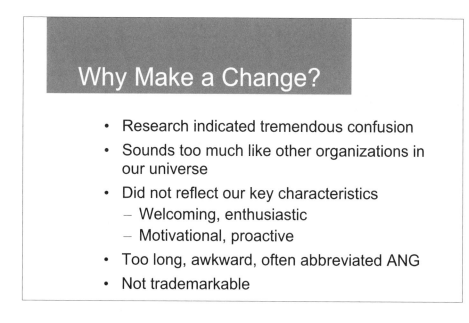

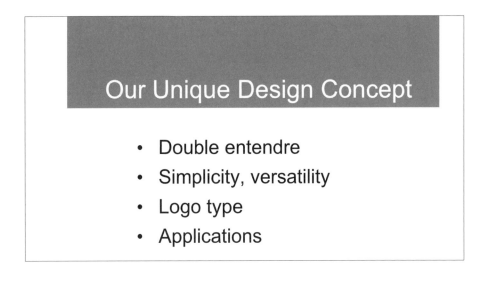

How We Did It or the Process Model

- Limited resources
- Learning curve
- Re-naming
- Choosing the right designers

Our Unique Design Concept

- Double entendre
- Simplicity, versatility
- Logo type
- Applications

GOVERNANCE MATTERS

GOVERNANCE **MATTERS**

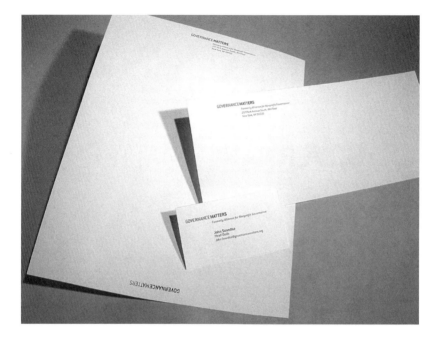

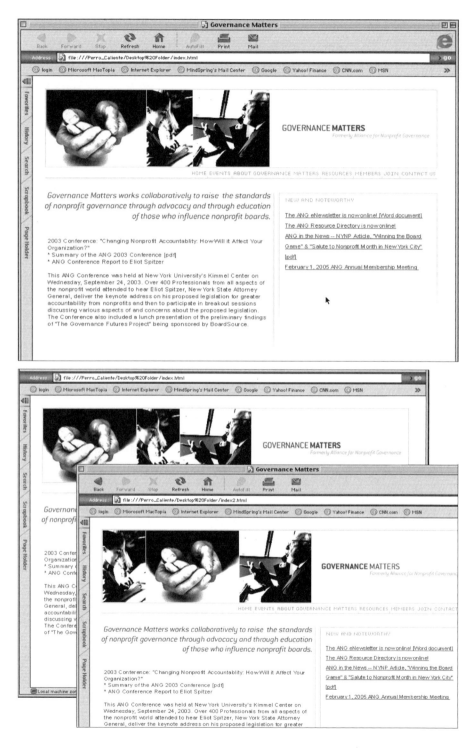

Orchestrating Change

- Launch plan to roll out our new name
- Partnering with you
- Vote to ratify

Brand Glossary

A   **Audience:** any defined group of people

B   **Brand:** a person's perception of a product, service, experience, or organization; the art and science of brand building. The brand has meaning beyond its functionality and exists primarily in the audiences' minds.

Brand audit: the process of reviewing all printed and electronic promotion and expressions of the brand, the end result of which is a chart or list of existing items for review and assessment.

Brand equity: the accumulated value of the brand's assets, both financially and strategically (including the products, name, colors, logo); the overall strength of a brand.

Brand image: a customer's mental picture of a product, service, or organization.

Brand manual: a document that articulates the parameters of the brand for members of the brand community; usually includes guidelines for formatting, imagery, nomenclature, typography, and color palette, as well as the brand positioning and the organization's mission statement.

Brand marketing: pushing beyond individual products or service benefits to fulfill a strategic core promise; looking past the tangible to the intangible, accommodating the audience's practical needs while reasoning with their deeper emotions.

Brand personality: the character of a brand as defined in human terms, such as MoMA = chic and refined, or P.S. 1 = maverick and edgy (see chapter 1).

Brand police: a humorous term for the stewardship's responsibility of strict compliance with the guidelines in the brand manual.

Brand promise: a stated or implied pledge that creates customer expectations and employee responsibilities, such as PBS's promise to eschew paid advertising in order to remain neutral (see chapter 1).

Brand qualities: the thoughts, feelings, associations, and expectations created by a brand identity.

Brand steward: the person on the brand team responsible for protecting the brand and keeping it on message.

Brand strategy: a plan for the systematic development of a brand in order to meet the organization's objectives.

Brand team: a committee formed to assess and guide an organization's brand-building process; sometimes called the creative council or brand council.

Branding: any effort or program to build a brand; the process of brand building.

Branding markers: the four assessment tools that are used to evaluate how successful a brand is currently: relevance, differentiation, esteem, and reputation (see chapter 2).

Buzz: the current public opinion about a subject, product, service, experience, or organization.

C **Color palette:** the limited range of colors selected to represent the brand in its applications.

Credit: the acknowledgment in print of the work of the creator(s).

D **Design:** to bring together strategic and creative processes to achieve a shared goal; a plan.

Design brief: a document that sets parameters for a brand-building project, including context, goals, processes, and budgetary constraints (also called a creative brief).

Differentiation: degree to which the brand is unique among others of its kind.

Documents audit: a review of all existing documents in order to determine what currently exists that represents the organization's current overall brand—anything from forms and fax cover sheets to the Web site and annual report.

E **Elevator pitch:** a one-sentence to three-paragraph recitation of a brand's purpose or market position, short enough to convey during a brief elevator ride; also called an "elevator conversation."

Esteem: the degree of confidence and respect afforded the organization by its primary audiences.

I **Identifier:** the line tied to the brand name that elaborates on the name, usually when the brand name is not descriptive in and of itself.

Identity: the outward expression of a brand, including its name, trademark, communications, and overall visual appearance; the way a brand is expressed visually and verbally.

Intellectual property: intangible assets protected by patents and copyrights; the legal discipline that specializes in the protection of brand assets (i.e., trade dress), including brand names, trademarks, colors, shapes, and sounds.

K **Kill fee:** the fee, agreed upon in advance, that would be received by the designer if the project were terminated at any point; the way the kill fee is calculated is spelled out in the terms and conditions of a written agreement.

L **Logo:** an abbreviation of "logotype," now applied broadly (if incorrectly) to all trademarks.

Logotype: a distinctive typeface or lettering style used to represent a brand name; a word mark.

Look and feel: the sensory experience of a brand's environment or communication.

M **Mark:** the symbol representing the brand.

Marketing: the process of developing, promoting, selling, and distributing a product or service; motivating people to become involved with your organization.

Markups: a carrying charge, usually 17.65 to 25 percent, for expenses incurred by the designer on the client's behalf; this is spelled out in the terms and conditions of a written agreement.

N **Nomenclature system:** a formal structure for naming related services, features, products, or benefits that link these things together as a family; the naming portion of an organization's brand architecture.

P **Plagiarism:** when a creator adapts and/or modifies the work of another creator without consent.

Positioning: the process of differentiating a product, service, or company in an audience's mind to obtain a strategic competitive advantage; the first step in building a brand.

Q **Qualitative research:** research designed to provide insight into the organization, through one-on-one interviews or focus groups.

R **Relevance:** the degree to which the brand is currently necessary, according to its audiences.

Reputation: the degree to which the audiences know the brand.

Rights transfer: the designer generally transfers the copyright to the client for the completed brand identity when payment is made in full, while retaining the rights to unfinished work.

S **SWOT analysis:** any conceptual tool that analyzes the organization's strengths, weaknesses, opportunities, and threats.

Symbol: a sign or trademark designed to represent a brand.

T **Tagline:** a sentence, phrase, or word used to summarize a market position, such as the American Red Cross's tagline, "Together we can save a life."

Trade dress: all the elements—such as color, typography, mark, imagery—that are collectively or individually identified as unique to the brand.

W **Work for hire:** a loophole (usually applied to staff members) in the U.S. copyright law which, if agreed to in a contract, makes the creator all but invisible; rights transfers, on the other hand, do not negate the creator's existence.

Work on speculation: when a creator is asked to work without an agreement that he or she will be paid and/or, in the case of pro bono projects, that the client is intending to take the work to completion.

Note: A nod to the AIGA's *The Dictionary of Brand* for inspiration and guidance.

About the Author

DK Holland is a writer, strategist and creative director who turned her attention to nonprofits after developing award-winning programs that included branding, licensing, promotion and product development for companies such as Mattel and Citicorp for over thirty years. She was, until 2001, a partner in The Pushpin Group, an internationally acclaimed design and illustration firm based in New York City.

DK says, "Now, more than ever, nonprofits need to compete for the public's attention to get their message respected and accepted. To accomplish this, we need to apply the best tools and tactics of big business to the business of nonprofits."

Currently, DK is the principal of DK Holland, LLC, a brand communications consultancy that works exclusively with nonprofits. Her clients include The Literacy Assistance Center, Sisters of Charity of New York, the Organization Development Network, Brooklyn Friends School, and the Buckminster Fuller Institute. DK recently led the rebranding team, along with other members, of Governance Matters (formerly the Alliance for Nonprofit Governance), and she serves on its board of directors. She was an executive director of a nonprofit for six years, and as a volunteer, founded two different nonprofits on which, in both cases, she served as chair for a number of years. She currently serves on three nonprofit boards.

She is an editor of *Communication Arts* magazine and the author/creative director of a dozen books on graphic design. In 1999 DK was awarded the Walter Hortens Distinguished Service Award by the Graphic Artists Guild National. She has been a judge for many design competitions in the graphic design industry. DK is currently a member of the AIGA.

DK teaches in the graduate school for nonprofit management of the New School. She lives in historic Fort Greene, Brooklyn in an early nineteenth-century building that was once a tanner's shop with her American cocker spaniel Walt Whitman and stray tiger cat, Frida Kahlo.

Index

through consistent
presentation, 5
brand steward
brand management by,
32, 42, 113
design brief circulation
by, 40
branding
America's use of, 136
by Apple Computer, 121
buy-in for, 75
evolution of, 128–131
funding for, 125–127
intangible benefits of,
137–138
LAC use of, 63–64
manipulation of,
129–130
nonprofits' need for, 56
for nonprofits v. profits,
117
photography for, 82
in religion, 134–135
uses of, 131–133
visual imagery in,
82–83, 101, 106–107
word and image use in,
101
branding materials
application of imagery
to, 83
success of, 46
types of, 46
branding process
availability of resources
for, 41
board of directors'
responsibility in, 42
brand steward impact
on, 42

brand strategies in,
43–45
consensus for, 31, 32
copy writer's job in, 43
design brief for, 20–21
design styles in, 43–44
designer role in, 49
emotional nature of, 80
goals for, 32
graphic design in, 44
graphic designer
influence on, 43
inclusive need for,
70–73
of LAC, 69
leadership of, 31–32, 42
nomenclature of, 38
organizational weak-
nesses in, 41
outside design
consultant in, 43
research and orienta-
tion of, 41–43
responsibility for, 31
style and strategy of,
43–45
team roles in, 42
team size in, 42
branding strategy
for American Red
Cross, 3
audience for, 34
benefits of, 8
budget for, 4, 22–23
C&G use of, 3–4
by committee, 24–27
communication of, 2
communication
vehicles for, 5
competition and, 46

definition of, 5
design elements for, 12
design success of, 3
design tools for, 5
differentiation through, 13, 23
educating graphic designers for, 36
effective use of, 2–3, 18
elements of, 20
expectations created by, 5
focus of, 13
fragmentation of, 25
implementation of, 4
ineffective use of, 7, 21
markers of, 6–7, 23–24
materials for, 4
mission and identity support of, 4
naming in, 36–40
nonprofit world weakness in, 7–8
nonprofits and outside consultants in, 21
origins of, 5
outreach efforts of, 2
PUPS' strengths in, 27–29
re-branding issues of, 15
roles needed in, 26
staff administration of, 4
branding team, designer impact on, 43
British Petroleum. See BP
Brooklyn Academy of Music. See BAM

C&G (Chermayeff & Geismar), 15
brand strategy by, 3–4
Chermayeff & Geismar. See C&G
Chermayeff, Ivan, 4
Communication Arts, 44, 109–110
copywriting
for brand identity, 81
branding process in, 43
with graphic designer, 102–103
nonprofits use of, 98, 102
outsourcing of, 105–106
tips for, 103–105
copyright law, 111
Crosby, Art, 99
Crosby, Bart, 34, 47–48

design
effective use of, 3
process of, 20–21
strategy in, 3, 12
structure and meaning from, 4
subjective opinions of, 76, 88
visual imagery in, 81–82
design brief
benefits of, 21, 27, 33
board review of, 24–25
brand steward impact on, 32
in branding process, 20–21

of PUPS, 29
refinement of, 80–81
simplicity advantages
for, 16
of Sisters of Charity of
New York, 76–77
subjective interpreta-
tion of, 76–80
of UPS, 64
usefulness of, 35–36
Web sites placement
of, 67

MABP (Make a Better
Place)
brand issues of, 11–12
case study of, 9–13
as client of Liska &
Associates, 56
logo effectiveness of,
11–12
mission of, 9
naming strategy of, 38
Maker a Better Place.
See MABP
mark. See logo
markups, 59
MoMA (Museum of
Modern Art)
brand campaign
success of, 18
branding issues of, 14
case study of, 13–19
design brief process of,
32–33
history of logo influ-
ence on, 17
MoMA QNS brand
issues for, 14

MoMA QNS (MoMA
Queens)
brand issues for MoMA
of, 14
branding purpose for,
16
logo of, 16
typography use by, 16
MoMA Queens. See
MoMA QNS
Munoz, Fernando, 12
Museum of Modern Art.
See MoMA

naming
AIGA strategy for,
37–38
of BP, 77
brand continuity
through, 38–39
feedback on, 37
with hybrids, 39
initialisms in, 38–39
issues of, 37–38
MABP strategy for, 38
MoMA issues with,
14
MoMA QNS issues of,
14
for nonprofits, 37
reasons for change in,
37
re-branding through,
39
nonprofits
attractions to, 56
audience for, 118
branding and design
needs of, 56

Books from Allworth Press

Allworth Press is an imprint of Allworth Communications, Inc. Selected titles are listed below.

Citizen Brand: 10 Commandments for Transforming Brands in a Consumer Democracy
by Marc Gobé (hardcover, 5½ × 8½, 288 pages, 46 b&w illus., $24.95)

Emotional Branding: The New Paradigm for Connecting Brands to People
by Marc Gobé (hardcover, 6¼ × 9¼, 352 pages, 134 b&w illus., $24.95)

The Entrepreneurial Age: Awakening the Spirit of Enterprise in People, Companies and Countries
by Larry C. Farrell (hardcover, 6¼ × 9¼, 352 pages, 17 figures, $24.95)

The Trademark Guide: A Friendly Handbook for Protecting & Profiting from Trademarks, Second Edition
by Lee Wilson (paperback, 6 × 9, 256 pages, $19.95)

The Copyright Guide: A Friendly Handbook for Protecting & Profiting from Copyrights, Third Edition
by Lee Wilson (paperback, 6 × 9, 256 pages, $19.95)

Dead Ahead: The Web Dilemma and the New Rules of Business
by Laurie Windham with Jon Samsel (hardcover, 6¼ × 9¼, 256 pages, 14 b&w figures, $24.95)

The Soul of the New Consumer: The Attitudes, Behaviors, and Preferences of e-Customers
by Laurie Windham with Ken Orton (hardcover, 6¼ × 9¼, 320 pages, 59 figures, $24.95)

NetSlaves® 2.0: Tales of "Surviving" the Great Tech Gold Rush
by Bill Lessard and Steve Baldwin (paperback, 6 × 9, 224 pages, $19.95)

Please write to request our free catalog. To order by credit card, call 1-800-491-2808 or send a check or money order to Allworth Press, 10 East 23rd Street, Suite 510, New York, NY 10010. Include $5 for shipping and handling for the first book ordered and $1 for each additional book. Ten dollars plus $1 for each additional book if ordering from Canada. New York State residents must add sales tax.

To see our complete catalog on the World Wide Web, or to order online, you can find us at
www.allworth.com.